Adventurous Pursuits
of a
Peninsular War
& Waterloo Veteran

The Story of Private James Smithies,
1st (Royal) Dragoons,
1807-15

Edited By
Gareth Glover

Published in 2011 by Ken Trotman Publishing.
Booksellers & Publishers
P.O.Box 505
Godmanchester
Huntingdon PE29 2XW
England
Tel: 01480 454292
Fax: 01480 384651
www.kentrotman.com

This edition © Gareth Glover 2011
Front cover illustration © Bob Marrion

All rights reserved. No part of this publication
may be reproduced, stored in a retrieval system or transmitted
in any form or by any means electrical,
mechanical or otherwise without first seeking the
written permission of the copyright owner and
of the publisher.

Design, layout and additional proofing
by Henry Hyde

Printed by MPG Biddles

ISBN 978-1-907417-28-3

ADVENTUROUS PURSUITS

OF A

PENINSULAR WAR

& WATERLOO VETERAN

THE STORY OF PRIVATE JAMES SMITHIES,
1ST (ROYAL) DRAGOONS,

1807-15

EDITED BY

GARETH GLOVER

I discovered this fascinating and rare journal of the life of Private James Smithies by accident, having stumbled over the transcript by Jhone Partington and her drive to gain further information regarding the life of her great-great-great-grandfather. Learning that his story had been published by his local newspaper as a serial following his tragic death, I contacted Jhone who kindly agreed to my publishing his story.

Memoirs by dragoons who fought in the Peninsular war are quite rare, which makes Smithies' account even more important. However, a word of caution must also be made. James Smithies apparently recounted his story shortly before his death, some fifty three years after the last events he describes had occurred and therefore, not surprisingly, he occasionally errs in his memory.

Public demand for memoirs of the 'Great War' – as the war against Napoleon was known until the First World War took on that epithet – was avid and a number had been published by the time of Smithie's death. Three major histories of the wars had also been published – Sir Charles Napier's History of the Peninsular War was completed in 1840; and Sir Archibald Alison's History of Europe from the Commencement of the French Revolution completed in 1860 and William Siborne's The Waterloo Campaign 1815 – and were thus available to interested parties. It is clear that Smithies knew and had access to at least Napier's and Alison's works; and there is at times clear evidence that he has utilised them to bolster his own knowledge. Some passages are clearly taken directly from these works, in other sections casualty figures and dates have clearly been utilised from these and Wellington's own published dispatches.

Smithies had probably – like many an old soldier of all ages – also learnt that a good yarn at the local public house would earn him a few free drinks from his eager audience. In such situations, the story grows with the telling, and actions at which his regiment could not have fought at are added to his tale; and general stories which passed around the army and were mentioned in numerous memoirs in some guise or another, were also claimed as his own.

His story must therefore rightly be treated with some caution and stories of the Battle of Salamanca, siege of San Sebastian and Battles of the Nivelle and Orthes can be dismissed as 'tall tales' as he could not possibly have been there.

However, it is unfair to even start to think of James Smithies' account as being historically worthless, even with all these faults. Because underneath all the flim-flam and tall tales, there is for those who bother to look properly, a thick vein of an honest account woven through his story and much that rings very true. For Smithies did not pull his punches and is at times brutally honest about some unsavoury incidents that he was either a participant or an eye-witness to much which must have both shocked and titillated his Victorian audience.

It is the only account I can recall where a soldier and his colleagues, who could not perform a mercy killing by cutting the throat of a fatally wounded friend; describe rolling him into a ditch and hastily burying him alive without any finer feeling. He was simply doing what his friend had wanted! His description of cavalry actions are not filled with heroics, but more the truth of confusion, lucky escapes and great relief to simply survive intact. And Waterloo, his last battle, is seen almost only through his own personal journey; his fear at encountering the cuirassiers and his tactic of riding close to them to prevent them having the room to make their deathly stab; his wounding and capture; his numerous brushes with death whilst being driven to the rear and eventual escape speak all too honestly of personal experience to have been added to – although his encounter with Napoleon himself is not likely – but it could simply be that he honestly 'thought' that it was Napoleon.

Overall, Smithies gives a clear insight into the life of a cavalry man – and his mind set amongst the interminable patrolling and very occasional fighting which the life of a soldier has always been – during Wellington's wars. It is very fortunate for us all therefore that the old and battered copy of the 'Adventurous pursuits of a Peninsular War Veteran' which had lain ignored until the time came to clear the contents and sell the old family home on the death of her remaining parent has now been saved for us by Jhone. James Smithies is undoubtedly an ancestor to be very proud of.

Gareth Glover, Cardiff, 2011

ORIGINAL INTRODUCTION

A word of introduction may not be improper in this place, of some circumstances connected with the subjoined. During last autumn it came to the knowledge of the writer that old Smithies, the veteran, had expressed a wish to make certain statements, or give certain descriptions of himself and the events in which he took so active a part, when he was a soldier. He had repeatedly stated that he had 'something to say' It was evident that a quick ear and ready hand were all that were wanted. The writer was not unknown to the family of the veteran, and, presenting himself for the purpose of chronicling the statements, found himself well received alike by the family and its head, the old soldier himself. Whatever merit there may be in the following narrative the writer is not concerned to enquire about. He only knows that it is Smithies' unaffected statement; that Smithies' was a man of probity; that he seemed to be heartily at work in the narration; that his names and dates and events are in singular accord with universally accepted histories of the events treated upon; and that the whole has been well received by a numerous class of readers, so much so that it has been earnestly asked for, and in the shape in which it is now presented to our readers.

LIFE & RECOLLECTIONS OF A PENINSULAR VETERAN AND WATERLOO HERO

Re-published from the Middleton Albion, of the 18th, January, 1868, and five successive Saturdays.

'For I had heard of battles, and longed to follow to the field some warlike lord.' Dr. Home's Play of Douglas[1].

In last week's Albion it was our painful duty to record a fatal accident to the old veteran, James Smithies, one of the few remaining who served under Wellington throughout his campaigns in Spain and Portugal, and afterwards at Waterloo. As a sketch of his life, and recollections of his military career, may be interesting to some of our readers, we here give as much as we are at present in possession of. He was born in the year 1787, and at an early age exhibited a great propensity for daring and dangerous feats, being almost a stranger to fear, and was what is

---

1 Douglas is a blank verse tragedy written by John Home and first played in Edinburgh in 1756.

now very commonly termed a little 'wild.' His parents, as indeed most of the inhabitants of Tonge[2] at that time, were weavers; but at the age of seventeen he became restless, and deserted the 'shet-burt un shuttle' to enlist in the army. He became a member of the Royal Artillery, but as his parents were strongly opposed to his leading the life of a soldier, they released him after he had been installed in the service only a few days. He returned home, but in less than a fortnight the careless, roving disposition again took possession of him, and about eleven o'clock one fine evening he arose from his bed, hastened to the house of John Oldham, who at that time lived on Lark Hill, Tonge[3], and was re-enlisted by him into the 1st Royal Dragoons, with which regiment he remained until he quitted the service.

About two years afterwards his regiment was ordered to Portugal, where they landed in the year 1809. They marched from Lisbon to Bussaco, and took part in an engagement at the latter place, He was also at the battles of Fuentes d'Onoro, Salamanca (twice)[4], Vitoria, the engagements in the Pyrenees mountains, a seven days' fight at Toulouse, in France, and lastly at Waterloo, where he was wounded and taken prisoner. He, however, made good his escape two days afterwards, and journeyed on foot to Brussels, where he lay in the hospital a short time. Before leaving Brussels two English literary gentlemen engaged him to escort them over the battle field, to explain the various points and positions occupied by the contending armies, and the plan of operations. The gentlemen informed him at the time that they were compiling a history of the battle, and it is supposed that they were the authors of Alison's 'History of the Campaigns against Napoleon,' for in that work it is stated that they (the authors) were conducted over the ground of Waterloo, a short time afterwards, by a British cavalryman who had taken part and been wounded in the battle. As Smithies answered the description thus given, it is probable that he was the person to whom it refers. After arriving in England once more he obtained his discharge, and settled down in his native village as a silk weaver. He was ultimately married, and has since reared a large family, most of whom are yet alive. In his later years, of course, he has been too feeble to follow any occupation, and has resided with several members of his

---

2   Tonge is now part of Middleton in Greater Manchester. In 1780 Tonge numbered only 70 inhabitants.

3   This was an area of Middleton, just off the Oldham Road; A Lark Hill Court stands on part of the site today. I must thank Pat Elliott, Community Librarian at Middleton Library for much local information on Lark Hill, Tonge and Jumbo.

4   There was only one battle at Salamanca, in 1812, however the Army did offer battle on the same ground later in the year, but the French did not attack.

family in Queen Street, Tonge. Although bowed down with age, up to the time of his unfortunate death his mental faculties were not in the least impaired, and it was really surprising with what clearness and accuracy he could remember names of persons and places, and dates of circumstances which occurred some fifty or sixty years ago.

Many are the times he has entertained a company with his reminiscences of days gone by, and never did he seem happier than when relating his adventures and hair-breadth escapes, or 'When the labours of the day were done, he handled his crutch, and showed how fields were won.'

For the last fifty-three years he has received a pension from the government, besides prize-money from various engagements in which he took part. He has composed a number of verses, chiefly relating to the exploits of the '1st Royals,' which we give below, not because they have any great claim to poetical merit, but there is something original contained in the sentiment, which is quite of a martial character. When the 1st Royal Dragoons were last in Manchester, he paid a visit to the barracks, and upon making himself known, the men raised him upon their shoulders, and carried him, as if in triumph, to the officers' quarters, cheering vociferously as they went along. The commanding officer was unfortunately absent, but the old veteran received a very cordial invitation to visit them again when the officer was there. Of course he was obliged to tell them what the regiment had gone through, and that he interested them very much there is no doubt. He was shown several relics of the regiment, and amongst them was the flag under which he himself had served for so many years. Before the old regiment set sail for Portugal, it numbered six hundred men, and Smithies, the last of them, has now gone to 'that bourne from whence no traveller returns.'

In concluding these few introductory remarks, we may say with all sincerity and reverence 'Soldier, rest! Thy warfare o'er, Dream of fighting fields no more: Sleep the sleep that knows not breaking, Morn of toil, nor night of waking.' Scott[5].

---

5   Taken from the poem written by Sir Walter Scott.
Soldier, rest! thy warfare o'er,
Sleep the sleep that knows not breaking:
Dream of battled fields no more,
Days of danger, nights of waking.
In our isle's enchanted hall,
Hands unseen thy couch are strewing,
Fairy strains of music fall,

We will now proceed to give his own version of his life as related by himself only a short time previous to his death.

Every sense in slumber dewing.
Soldier, rest! thy warfare o'er,
Dream of fighting fields no more:
Sleep the sleep that knows not breaking,
Morn of toil, nor night of waking.

No rude sound shall reach thine ear,
Armour's clang, or war-steed champing,
Trump nor pibroch summon here
Mustering clan, or squadron tramping.
Yet the lark's shrill fife may come
At the day-break from the fallow,
And the bittern sound his drum,
Booming from the sedgy shallow.
Ruder sounds shall none be near,
Guards nor warders challenge here,
Here's no war-steed's neigh and champing,
Shouting clans or squadrons stamping.

Huntsman, rest! thy chase is done,
While our slumbrous spells assail ye,
Dream not, with the rising sun,
Bugles here shall sound reveillé.
Sleep! the deer is in his den;
Sleep! thy hounds are by thee lying;
Sleep! nor dream in yonder glen,
How thy gallant steed lay dying.
Huntsman, rest; thy chase is done,
Think not of the rising sun,
For at dawning to assail ye,
Here no bugles sound reveillé.

SMITHIES' NARRATIVE

I was first enlisted in July 1804, at the Hare and Hounds Inn[6], Tonge, in the artillery; I was sworn in at Cheadle[7] by a magistrate, but in consequence of my having been sworn-in in less than twenty four hours, my friends interfered and advised me to return home, which I did. I therefore went back to my weaving; but it was not long before I wanted to be off again, and in a fortnight after I came home, I went to 'Jack of Owdham's' house at eleven o'clock at night and asked him to list me. Jack was the recruiting sergeant for this district and lived at the top of Little Park, Tonge. He was in bed when I knocked at the door, so he got up, put his head out of the window and asked my business, which I of course told him. He let me in and finding he had not a shilling in his pocket, he went upstairs, awoke his mother to borrow one, with which he enlisted me. I was sent to Ipswich[8] by bus[9], and ordered to join the First Regiment or the Royal Dragoons. After remaining at that place about a month we went to Colchester[10], where I was taken ill with cholera. I was sent home on a furlough of ten weeks, and after I returned we proceeded to York[11], where our headquarters were situate at that time; my troop, however, was sent on to Sheffield, where we stayed a month. From thence we went to Newcastle upon Tyne; and I remember it was at Christmas time, in the year 1805[12] we returned to Woodbridge, near Ipswich, and in a few weeks made the march through Newcastle upon Tyne, Morpeth, Berwick upon Tweed, to Edinburgh, where we were quartered for a year and a few months[13]. Afterwards we went to Port Patrick, and embarked for Donaghadee, on the north-west coast of Ireland, and marched through Belfast, Lisburn, Enniskillen, to Dundalk[14], which was the headquarters. I there joined the

---

6   The Hare and Hounds still stands on Oldham Road, Middleton.

7   It is strange that he was sworn at Cheadle which is a number of miles south of Manchester.

8   The regiment was stationed at Ipswich from April to November 1804; if he was there only a month he must have arrived around early October.

9   A passenger coach.

10 The Royals wintered at Colchester.

11 The regiment proceeded to York in April 1805.

12 1804 is written in the text but is a clear error, the regiment marching to Woodbridge at Christmas 1805.

13 In March 1806 they marched to Edinburgh and remained there until January 1807 when they sailed to Ireland. They actually therefore remained in Edinburgh about nine months.

14 The regiment had its headquarters at Dundalk with detached troops at Belturbet, Lisburn,

band, which was reformed, and had for a time been broken up. The instrument I played was the clarionet. We went to Dublin[15], when we received orders to go abroad. We had got on board with all our horses, stores, and accoutrements, when the order was countermanded and we disembarked accordingly[16]. The 23rd horse[17] was ordered to embark in the ship which was to have taken us, and they went in our stead. It's very remarkable that this regiment was very badly cut up in the first engagement they took part in, which was at Talavera in Spain, and that might have been our luck if we had gone. We went from Dublin to Clonmel[18], and there we were stationed a few months. Lord Montagu[19] was our commanding officer, and I was his orderly, and always a great favourite with him. I remember one evening I was on sentry [duty] in front of the barracks, when a lady came up to me and said, 'Here, common man, where is Lord Montagu?' I said, 'He's in the barrack, common lady!' It proved to be Lady Montagu, and I suppose she felt her dignity insulted by being thus replied to by only a 'common' man. The result was she mentioned the matter to certain petty officers who were only too glad to be of service to her ladyship, and I was ordered to be placed in the guardroom for the night, and to be brought for trial in the morning on the charge of having 'grossly insulted' the commanding officer's wife. I did not feel put out of the way about this, as I knew Lord Montagu would look at it in the right light when I gave my version of the affair. Well, morning came; I was brought up, when his lordship exclaimed, 'Hollo, Smithies, is it you; what have they to say against you, I wonder.' I told him how Lady Montagu had accosted me when enquiring for him, and as soon as he had heard it he said, laughingly, 'Release him; it served her right for speaking to a man in that manner.'

We received orders to proceed to Cork, where we embarked for Portugal on

---

Monaghan, Sligo, Enniskillen and Londonderry.

15 The regiment marched to Dublin in June 1808 with detachments at Carlow and Athy.

16 The regiment had embarked at Cork but news of the evacuation of the army following the Battle of Corunna caused the order to be countermanded.

17 The 23rd Light Dragoons went to Spain and lost heavily when their charge at Talavera ran into a hidden ravine, causing a number of injuries.

18 The regiment moved to Clonmel in April 1809 and remained there until August.

19 Later comments make it clear that he means Captain William Montague, who commanded his squadron, but he was not from nobility. Did he mix him up with Lord William Montagu (son of the Duke of Manchester) who appeared in Army Lists from 1826 thinking that they were the same person? I must thank Ron McGuigan for his help in solving this issue.

the 3rd September 1809[20], to join Wellington's army. James Dyson, of Bradshaw Fold, Jumbo[21], was in our regiment, and when we were going on this voyage he composed the following verses, which were sung by nearly everyone aboard after we landed:

> Come all you jovial Royal Dragoons,
> The truth if you would know,
> The order now to us has come,
> To face our daring foe.
> Unto the 'Cove of Cork,' my boys,
> We quickly must repair,
> From thence on board the transport ships
> For Portugal to steer.
>
> It was a painful sight to see,
> When we came to Cork Hill,
> Our men so soon should fall a-drinking,
> And women cry their fill.
> To see men and wives at parting,
> T'would grieve your heart full sore,
> Crying 'Farewell, dearest husband,
> We ne'er shall see you more.'
>
> Now early on the next morning,
> Before the break of day,
> When the trumpets briskly sounded,
> Our men gave loud hurrahs.
> We marched to the Cove, my boys,
> As you shall understand,
> To cross the briny ocean
> And leave Hibernia's land.
>
> On the third day of September,

---

20 Eight troops of eighty men each embarked at Cork for Portugal under Colonel the honourable George de Grey.

21 Jumbo is an old name for Middleton Junction which was in the area of Middleton around present day Grimshaw Lane.

12

Just by the break of day,
A signal gun was duly fired
To get us under weigh.
Then we weighed our anchors briskly,
And we put out to sea,
And in ten toiling days and nights
We crossed the Bay of Biscay.

When we crossed the Bay of Biscay
The seas ran mountains high,
We were forced to haul our topsails in,
Or else our yards would fly.
For the foaming billows blew so high,
It would your hearts surprise,
Sometimes when down in valleys low,
And then tossed mountains high.

On the twelfth day of September,
Just as the day appeared,
Our convoy gave the signal
Some harbour we were near.
Then up the river called Tagus,
Our gallant fleet did steer,
And in two hours' time, my boys,
New Lisbon town appeared.
We sailed past Fort St. Julian
And Belem Castle, too,
And then we dropped our anchor,
And brought our ships in-to.
Then we quickly slung our horses
And hove them overboard,
And to the town of Belem
They were forced to swim ashore.

Our officers were valiant,
Our men in spirits high,
And all were anxious for the orders
Our enemy to try.

Brave General Slade commanded us,
A man of courage bold,
He vowed that with his Royal Brigade
He ne'er would be controlled.

So now our voyage it is o'er,
And friends we've left behind,
We'll toast our wives and good sweethearts
In bumpers of good wine.
Here's health to each jolly Dragoon,
The infantry also,
That fights in Spain and Portugal
Against the country's foe.

We remained in Lisbon from the 12th of September, 1809, to the 1st of January, 1810[22], when we marched to Santarem, where we were joined by the 14th Light Dragoons[23]. We were then ordered to advance to the borders of Spain[24], where, after meeting the foe, we retreated to draw them out to battle[25]. We continued to retreat until we came to Bussaco, where we faced each other and fought a pitched battle, which lasted for several days[26]. The Sierra de Bussaco, which presented an advantageous position for the resistance of the enemy, is a range of mountains, stretching from the north about eight miles to the river Mondego, where it terminated abruptly with almost a perpendicular fall. It was very steep indeed; here and there covered with pine trees, and stood about 250 feet from the ground

---

22 The regiment occupied Belem barracks on 12/13 September and did remain there until January 1810.

23 General Slade commanded a cavalry brigade consisting of the 1st (Royal) Dragoons and the 14th Light Dragoons.

24 The regiment moved to Nisa in the Alemtejo in February 1810.

25 The Royals were moved to Belmonte in the Beira when the French advanced to threaten Ciudad Rodrigo where they arrived on 8 May 1810. With the impossibility of relieving Ciudad Rodrigo becoming obvious, the Royals left Belmonte on 9 June for Vila Velha do Rodao, on 1 July they moved to Vila do Touro (just north of Sabugal) and at the end of July to Alverca da Beira.

26 The Battle on the Sierra de Bussaco occurred on 27 September lasted only one day and although victorious Wellington was forced to retire further into Portugal by the larger French force turning his position at Bussaco the day after the battle. Being on a rugged slope, the battle was a purely infantry and artillery affair and no cavalry were engaged.

in the front. At the highest point in the ridge, about two miles to the north, was a table land, occupied by the Carmelite convent of La Trappe, and to the left of that was a village called [San] Antonio de Cantara. In front of Bussaco there was a long line of hills or heights, from the first of which it was separated by a wooded chasm of great depth, but so narrow that a 12-pounder could range to the highest of the hilly points upon the opposite ridge. We had now taken up our position on this side of those heights nearest to Bussaco, with the French directly opposite us, and the valley I have just mentioned was between us. On the 25th September they opened a brisk cannonade on us, and some smart skirmishing took place between the French light troops and ours; in the course of the night, some of their skirmishers stole up among the pine trees, and determined to establish themselves close to the pickets of the light division; but they were quickly driven back. On the night of the 26th the English line of battle was formed, 25,000 British and about the same number of Portuguese soldiers lay at the back of the mountain, the Portuguese having been brigaded in proportion to one Portuguese battalion to two of the English. Wellington so arranged this in order to prevent them from throwing down their arms and flying in disorder as they had done before upon meeting the enemy. Neither the Spaniards nor the Portuguese would fight unless they were placed in the middle of a lot of our men, when they had no alternative but to strike for their lives or die. Our regiment was held in reserve[27], and we were posted at the convent, where Wellington had established his head quarters. The army had been laid out to the best advantage, and every preparation made for a battle by the 27th, and we expected they would attack us on the following day. When the darkness had come over us on the same night (the 27th), it was a grand sight to look at the thousands of camp fires on both sides of the hill. In our camp the old veteran soldiers who were accustomed to war and scenes of excitement, slept soundly in their beds, whilst the young soldiers (such as myself) who were to witness and take part in a battle for the first time, were kept awake by the grandeur of the scene before us, which it would be impossible to describe. The night, too, was of a different complexion to those which had usually attended Wellington's great victories: storms, attended with intense thunder, lightning, and rain, were the usual forerunners of all his great and glorious battles in the Peninsula, and the case was the same at Waterloo. His battles also were generally fought on a Sunday. It was not extraordinary, then, that a feeling should run through our army that we were about to experience a reverse. Stormy nights were called 'Wellington nights,' but though the night before the battle of Bussaco

---

27 Slade's Brigade was held in Reserve behind the convent and was not engaged as Smithie states.

was not a 'Wellington night,' the air was cold and piercing. When the day was just beginning to break, about two o'clock in the morning, a musket shot from the enemy was heard, followed by another and another, until every bush and tuft on the face of the Serra seemed to be alive with fire.

The entire allied army were instantly under arms and the fight began. I cannot explain the details of the battle, as I was with my regiment who were defending the pass to the convent. After the battle's roar had ceased, and the enemy had retreated we had time to look about us. Long trails of dying and dead, wounded men with broken arms and bleeding carcasses, marked the lines of their flight. The clusters of rocks presented a curious sight too, but it was a very sad one. In many of the niches we saw dead Frenchmen in the position they had fought in, some were sitting upright, others with their heads resting on the points of the rocks, apparently in the act of taking aim, whilst on the opposite hills the bodies of the brave defenders were strewn in every direction. Being the first engagement I had ever been in, this sight was new to me. The French reported that they had lost 2,000 men, 3,000 were wounded, and they also lost 300 in prisoners. The loss of British and Portuguese was only 197 killed, a little over 1,000 wounded, besides which there were 68 missing[28]. We had a deal of fun afterwards when we heard of the French commander's boast the day before the battle that 'he would drive the leopard (Wellington) into the sea,' to which it was said Wellington replied, 'If he do I shall beat him' and beat him he did, and right soundly too. The enemy on leaving Bussaco fell back on Torres Vedras[29], pursued by our army. Here we had another engagement with them, but as our regiment did not take part in it, for we were posted at some distance from it, I cannot tell you much about it. After the engagement of Torres Vedras the French retreated, in the same manner as they did at Bussaco, and did not come to a stand until they reached Santarem. As we pursued them we came upon Marshal Ney with his corps, and Montbrun with the cavalry at Tomar; we drove them forward, and then put up for the night. There was no available space for camping, and so we were billeted, a few to every

---

28 Smithie is close in his estimates as Oman states that at Bussaco the French lost 844 killed and 3,400 wounded (there is no record of missing/prisoners); Wellington's forces lost 200 killed, 1001 wounded and 51 missing.

29 Smithie's memory fails him here; for it was Wellington who was forced to retreat not the French. They did retreat to the Lines of Torres Vedras, which consisted of two defensive lines built across the Lisbon Peninsula from the sea to the Tagus. Consisting of hundreds of forts, abbatis and scarped hills, the lines were too strong for the French to assault and they eventually retreated when starvation and disease had taken a terrible toll on their ranks.

house in the town. I remember very well the place that I got sent to, along with a few of my comrades; it was something like a vault or wine cellar. Everything was in darkness when we got there, and we had nothing to strike a light with, so we had to be content with making ourselves as comfortable as possible. We were looking about as well as we could in the dark to find any furniture on which to lay our weary limbs, when one of our number, who was groping near the empty fire grate, touched the form of a man standing erect against the mantlepiece, but which now fell flat upon the floor. We knew he must be dead, and having no light we put him on one side until morning came, so that we could see who and what he was. I ought to have told you that the house we were in had been deserted by its owner, very likely on the approach of the soldiers. In going across the room, which was a pretty large one, I myself stumbled over another body, and this we served like the other, until we could 'take stock' of him better. We found our way to the wine barrels, and discovering some we could tap, we had our fill, being greatly fatigued and very thirsty indeed. In the morning we rose early, and our first thing was to examine the bodies we had come across the night before. We found them both to be French foot soldiers, who must have taken refuge in the house and been shot by our soldiers, and whilst three of us were overhauling them for anything they might have, a fourth, who was on the top of the wine barrel seeing how much wine there was left, and calculating very likely how long it would 'last' us, shouted out that he had found another Frenchman; and sure enough it was true, for we pulled another body out of the barrel by the hair of the head. This barrel had no top on, and we supposed he had leaped into it to escape detection, and been drowned in the wine. And this was the wine we had been drinking with such a relish! It was the strangest circumstance of its kind that I ever saw during the whole time I was a soldier. We were next encamped at Santarem, with Massena and his army on the side nearest Spain. It was now coming on for winter, and it would have to be decided whether the French should be allowed to encamp in Portugal, or, if possible, we were to drive them out of the country.

Various rumours were afloat in the army to the effect that the French were meditating a retreat, and to discover the truth of this rumour several of the commanding officers went out upon a reconnoitering tour our chief officer went, and took me as his orderly. We could see by the telescope the place where the French had been encamped, but could perceive no signs of life whatever, though the sentries seemed to be posted in their usual places. We approached these sentries as cautiously as possible, not wishing to attract any attention, and when we got nearer to them we noticed that they continued to face us in the same manner as when we first saw them. My officer ordered me to challenge the one nearest to us, which I did, but received no reply. I thought I'd make the fellow either speak or run, so I charged him at full gallop, and cut him in two, but great was our surprise to find, instead of a living sentry, it was a dummy on horseback stuffed with straw. We discovered other dumb sentries placed along the line. It was found that under cover of darkness, and during a very heavy mist which hung over the mountain sides, they had broken up their position and beat a retreat. Wellington's army was immediately on the move, and pursued the enemy, who fell back rapidly, and did not make a stand until they reached far into Spain. 'Whilst we were encamped at Santarem I saw a great deal both in camp amongst the soldiers, and of the Portuguese and Spaniards who inhabited the place. There was great distress amongst the population, occasioned by the raids which the French had made on their property. They applied for aid to Wellington, and he generously opened a kind of relief fund, besides making an appeal for support to the people of England. We got to know this from the English newspapers which arrived every mail. He raised a subscription in the army: the officers subscribed liberally, and every private sacrificed one day's pay; by this arrangement we raised no less a sum than £8,000[30]. I very often shared my rations with the poor people who had been driven from their homes, and robbed of everything they possessed by the French soldiery, for I felt very sorry for them. We had plenty of life in camp, and at this time we had an abundance of provisions, which was not always the case, as you will hear after, and as much wine as we choose to take; in fact it seemed to be more plentiful than water. We were allowed plenty of time to look about us, too, provided we kept within the lines; and every day there was some kind of a gala or recreation being held. I have before told you of the dumb sentries we had discovered, and which had been placed there in order to throw Wellington off his guard, and to mask the retreat of the French army. It could not be decided at first whether they had retreated to draw us out of our strong position, or whether they really were on the retreat. Scouring parties were sent out, and some of these came up with the rear guard of the enemy, which they found to be retreating very rapidly towards the borders of Spain.

When this decisive intelligence came the army was put on the move, and pushed forward with all haste. But Wellington had a deal to contend with, for the Portuguese army ran short of provisions, and the government of Portugal either could not or would not send supplies, I am inclined to think the latter. They seemed to think they should be maintained out of the provisions sent for the British army, because we had come to help their army to drive the French out

---

30   It would be an incredible sum if true, as in modern terms it would equate to £272,000.

of their country! During the last nine months no less than ten thousand of the Portuguese soldiers had deserted their standards through want, and returned to their homes; and to prevent the total abandonment of their colours, Wellington ordered them to be fed out of the provisions which had been sent for us. But we had no right to complain of this so long as there was plenty for us, and we knew that neither ourselves nor the Portuguese could perform our duties, and go through the hardships we had, without sufficient food. When there was a great army together in a very little space, you may be sure we got up 'stirs' now and then to create a bit of excitement. We had discussion classes[31], at which a great many used to attend, but they generally broke up with fighting one among another.

There were prayer meetings and different sorts of religious gatherings held very often, I should think four or five times a week. Two of them were Methodists, one of which belonged to the Foot Guards, and was held at Cartaxo, a small town adjoining; another among the cavalrymen, which was presided over by a private named Asker. The men met in the evening, and sang psalms; and Sergeant Stephens preached occasionally, after a fashion of his own. Some of the officers did not like these carryings on, and they complained to Wellington, but the good old general only said that it was a more innocent way of spending our time than many other habits we were addicted to, but, at the same time he thought that from the way in which some of them had been ended up it might become otherwise than innocent. We also received and sent challenges between ourselves, to sword or bayonet combat; though it was merely as a trial of skill and not with any intention to hurt anyone. One day, a big burly Scotchman, in one of the Hussar regiments, challenged the best man in our regiment to come forward and try chances with him. Lord Montagu selected two of our number – myself and a comrade – and on 'tossing up' it fell to my lot to tackle him. I was considered to be about the most expert swordsman in 'the Royals' and I suppose it was on that account I was picked out. As I have before stated my antagonist was a tall fellow with plenty of muscle. When he saw me advancing towards him (I was thin and rather low in stature) he said, 'And am I to fight a leetle devil like you?' 'Yes, you old whiskey-barrel,' I said, upon which he seemed rather riled, and instantly crossed swords. He showed his superior strength, but skill and dexterity were wanted, and not altogether muscle. We were engaged for fully half an hour, during which period I placed him hors de combat several times. It ended by my taking off the top part of his left ear, when he laid down his sword, saving ' Hoot,

---

31 An interesting diversion in camp which I have not encountered before.

man, I didna think ye could ha done that for me.' Whilst at this place I heard tell of an English merchant coming from about Manchester; he was doing a large business in selling blankets, rugs, and other things that the troops were in need of to protect them on those cold, chilly nights. Coming from so near my native village, I went to speak with him, and he told me his name. He was brother to Mr. Ashton, who is now one of the magistrates in Middleton. The two contending armies had now been face to face with each other for nearly four months, and the only movement on either side was made by the French General Junot, on the 19th January, in 1811, on Rio Maior, for the purpose of ascertaining whether the British and their allies were being concentrated at Alcoentre. But it appears some of the Portuguese 'turncoats' had told Massena, the commander-in-chief of the French, that we were about to attack him with a view to the relief of Badajoz, and thinking he could not maintain his position, he determined to retreat. It was said that disease was very prevalent in his army; they were almost starving for want of provisions, and there had been great desertions in consequence, so that his force had dwindled down considerably. The number of deserters was so numerous that they formed themselves into a little army, which they arranged in regular companies, and called themselves 'the Eleventh Corps'; they elected their own general officers and subalterns. It consisted of more than 1,600 men, who very frequently attacked the parties of the French when returning from a 'scouring tour,' loaded with provisions, and made the prisoners join their band. They took up their quarters between Caldas [da Rainha] and Alcobaca in full sway as a desperate army of professional robbers. They seemed to terrify the inhabitants a great deal, and in that way became very powerful; but in consequence of their attacks on the French foraging parties, Massena sent a small force against them; they fought with great desperation, but were surrounded at last, overpowered, and forced to lay down their arms[32]. Their leaders were shot, and the men were again sent to their regiments, as if nothing had taken place.

But to return to the retreating enemy. Another cause that induced Massena to retreat was very likely because of the arrival in the Tagus of a large fleet of transport ships from England with a reinforcement of about 8,000 men, which had long been expected, and as soon as they had joined us he knew we should commence active operations. The French commenced their arrangements for a retreat in the end of February. They had for some time been gradually passing

---

32 The story of the marauding sergeant 'Marechal Chaudron' and his band of deserters, or 'fricoteurs' has now become legend and the truth probably much distorted; but there clearly was such a band. See Oman Volume IV pp 12 and Marbot pp 418-9.

their sick and baggage to Tomar, and destroying all ammunition and guns they could not carry away in a hurry. They then showed a bold front, and made a great display of attempting to pass the Zezere, a small river running north of Tomar, but it was only a move on their part to throw the British off their guard, and matters having been so arranged, the French retired on the night of the 5th of March from Santarem and its neighbourhood. The morning following, the appearance of the motionless sentinels reminded us of the ruse they had adopted before, and we were not long in getting to know that they had abandoned their position. The English army was in instant pursuit. General Hill's division was sent across the Tagus to harass the enemy's movements, and for the purpose of protecting the town of Abrantes, on the banks of the river. Beresford was ordered to advance to the relief of Badajoz, with the third, fourth, and fifth divisions, and a lot of Portuguese. The chief part of Massena's army was concentrated round Abrantes, and his line of retreat was down by the valley of the Mondego. The British advance guard, in the pursuit, was composed of the light division, the regiment I was in, and the first German Hussars, who took more than 200 prisoners. On the 9th, Montbrun's cavalry, and a great number of infantry was found to be in front of Pombal, and it was through this town that Massena beat such a hasty retreat on the night of the 11th, taking Montbrun with him, but leaving a body of troops in the castle to defend it. The following morning, the 95th Rifles, and the German regiment, drove them out in such a hurry that they had not even time to blow up the bridge leading to it, though it was already mined.

On the 12th, Ney, with the rearguard, took up a strong position between Pombal and Redinha, and he laid his force out so well as to make us believe he had a very powerful force. We immediately got orders to attack the enemy, and in less than an hour his right was carried by the 52nd regiment, the 95th Rifles, the 3rd Cacadores; and I believe there was a company of the 43rd. In the meantime, General Picton, with the 3rd division, had seized the wooded heights that protected his left. But though his (Ney's) position was thus laid open, he maintained his ground, from the conviction that the English were deceived as to his strength; and such was really the case, so skillfully had he masked his force. Our regiment did not take any very particular part in this affray, (though we witnessed it,) as the hilly nature of the ground prevented the cavalry from rendering much assistance. There was a stoppage for about an hour until we could concentrate a sufficient force to ensure success. Then three shots from our centre gave the signal for the advance, when, in less than it takes to tell it, the wood seemed to sparkle with bayonets, and the whole army was on the march; while horsemen and guns, starting at the same time from the left wing and centre, charged under a general volley from the French battalions. A dense cloud of smoke enveloped the enemy for a short time, and when it rose and we could see through it, no enemy was visible! It appears that they had rapidly withdrawn, and got as far as the village of Redinha before our cavalry could reach them, and so rapidly did they retreat that the best we could do was to fire on the rearmost of the fugitives. On the following day the pursuit was resumed, and the English advanced guard reached Condeixa [a Nova] about ten o'clock in the morning, but as the position we had taken up was not passable in front, being very marshy, and that the right of the heights on which he was posted was protected by a palisade, and breastworks thrown up on either side of the hollow by which it could be approached, Picton, with his third division, was sent by a 'roundabout' path through the Sierra de Anciao mountains for the purpose of turning the left flank of the enemy. As soon as Massena saw him coming round by the end of this mountain, about eight miles from his position, the whole camp was thrown into confusion. We soon saw a thick cloud of smoke rise from Condeixa, and their columns were at the same time observed hurrying towards Casal Nova, which would be about three or four miles, something like going from here to Oldham.

Our advanced guard pushed on with great eagerness, but it could not get along very well, in consequence of the town having been set fire to, and they had cut down trees and thrown them across the roads. They also kindled a lot of fires to conceal their flight in the smoke. But our soldiers were so eager to catch up with them, that a few of the skirmishers and some of the cavalry got into Massena's headquarters, and nearly captured the French Marshal, who escaped by disguising himself, and scrambling over the mountains by night to get to his army. We followed him towards Celorico [da Beira], on the right side of the Mondego. Here we took about 100 prisoners, and killed a great many. From the movements of the French it was now believed that they were going to make a stand, and in order to prevent this five columns of infantry, with the cavalry, which were supported on the wings by the Third Division and the Portuguese militia, under Generals Trant and Wilson; in the centre by the Fifth and Seventh Divisions; attacked them from as many points on the Guarda mountain, in the form of a semicircle, but so arranged that they would all meet at one point near the citadel, and at the same time overlapping the enemy's flanks. As soon as Massena saw this force, in the greatest hurry and confusion they abandoned this almost impregnable situation as if they had seen an apparition. They crossed the Coa, but not before several of their brigades had been cut off, and baggage, ammunition, and stores, as well as a portion of the property of which the Portuguese had been robbed, fell into our hands. They then halted, and we could see by their fires that they were cooking, and as we had had nothing to eat that day, our commanding officer conceived the idea of surprising them, and capturing some of their provisions. This was no sooner planned than carried out, and, although we were greatly fatigued, I can assure you we went at it with a hearty goodwill, for there was a prospect of a good dinner if we succeeded. Well, we did attack them, and I suppose the French did not perceive us, as they were so busy eating, until we were directly on them. As soon as they saw our soldiers advancing to attack them (and they were not prepared to fight), they gathered up their arms and fled in the greatest possible confusion, leaving us their cooked dinners just ready for demolishing. We drove them a few miles beyond here, and then returned to partake of the dinners which the French had cooked for themselves. I don't think they'd exactly like it, but I can assure you we did, for it was first class. The dishes were very tolerable; there were plenty of sauces, and such like, but hunger was the best sauce that improved the dinner for us. The reason that our whole army was without provisions was because our pursuit of the French had been so rapid that our provision wagons could not keep up with us, and we could not collect any food from the places we had to pass through, being rather mountainous in that part of the country. But when the French left Santarem every man was supplied with bread for a fifteen days' march, and they had collected large quantities by plundering on their march. After receiving refreshments, and allowing time for the stores and provisions to come up with us, we started again, and very quickly came upon them. In this manner; it being our duty to allow him no rest he was obliged to seek safety in constant flight. When he reached Sabugal his pursuer was quickly upon his track; and although Massena had taken up a very strong position, Wellington quickly dislodged him from his stronghold. Here the French marshal determined on making a last effort to maintain his hold of Portugal, and perhaps to avoid the disgrace of having been driven from it himself, instead of having fulfilled his boast that he would 'drive us into the sea in less than three months from his entering Portugal.' His head-quarters were at Alfaiates; his left had one flank on a height above the bridge and town of Sabugal, and the other extending upon the road to Alfaiates as far as a lofty ridge which commanded all the approaches to Sabugal, from the fording places of the Coa, which were a little above the town. On the 1st of April the English army was concentrated on the right bank of the Coa, and at daybreak the 43rd Regiment was in motion to drive the enemy from his position.

It was the object of the English commander-in-chief to cut off the 6th corps at

Roveria [Ruvina?] before help could arrive to it[33]. For this purpose he disposed of his army as follows: that different divisions should pass the Coa at the same time by three of the fords, and by the bridge of Sabugal, to attack the enemy in front, flank, and rear at the same time. We cavalrymen, who formed the right of the British position, forded the river by the upper Coa, the Light Division a little lower down above Sabugal; the Third still lower; and the Fifth, with the artillery, by the bridge of Sabugal ; all to direct our force on the position of the 6th corps. But this scheme was spoiled by the clumsy blundering of Sir William Erskine[34], our commander at that attack. He did not put the columns in the right direction; the brigades were not held together, and he carried off the cavalry. Besides this we had to contend with the weather, which had now become exceedingly wet, and rendered the roads very muddy, and made it very difficult to go through our different movements. Beckwith's brigade, consisting of the 43rd, four companies of the 95th, and three companies of the 3rd Cacadores, were the first to ford the river, and with some of Erskine's bungling, they were ordered to attack before the other columns had advanced to their respective battle stations to support him. By this movement he was unconsciously advancing against more than 12,000 infantry, supported by cavalry and artillery. They had no sooner driven in the enemy's pickets and reached the top of the hill, than they were forced back upon the 43rd by overwhelming numbers; and at the same moment, the fog clearing off, exhibited to Beckwith the peril he was placed in. He, however, resolved to meet it, and make the best of it. Heading a fierce charge, he beat back the enemy, and gained the top of the hill again, when he was attacked in front and flank by fresh troops, supported by cavalry, while they fired two guns at musket range with a deadly discharge on his little band; at the same time the fire of the French musketry was increasing to a perfect storm of bullets. He protected himself on a small stone enclosure until the 52nd Regiment (men who had never yet met their match) came to his assistance. The French now began to fall very fast. A howitzer was taken from them, and the English skirmishers of the 52nd falling back upon the main body of their regiment, the whole of the men instantly forming line behind a stone wall, overthrew with their rolling fire everything that came in their way. The French general Reynier soon saw that his partial attacks would not do, and accordingly advanced a column of 6,000 men, supported by cavalry and artillery; but Captain Hopkins, with a company of the 52nd[35],

---

33 It was actually the 2nd Corps that was isolated at Sabugal.

34 Major General Sir William Erskine, was temporarily in charge of the advance guard.

35 The only Hopkins at this action was Lieutenant John Hopkins of 43rd Foot.

mounted a small eminence, commanding the ascent by which the enemy was advancing with two volleys, throwing them into confusion, immediately charged them with the bayonet. At the same time, the leading brigade, under General Colville[36] of the 3rd Division, came out of the woods on the enemy's right, and opened a destructive fire on that flank; whilst the 5th, having carried the bridge, was going up the heights on the same flank; and at the same moment our cavalry was advancing on the high ground on the left of the enemy. A violent storm of hail now came on, and Reynier, seeing that he was nearly surrounded, retreated rapidly to Rendo, and afterwards to Alfaiates. Besides leaving us in possession of the battle field, the French lost about 1,500, of whom 300 were prisoners[37]. Our loss scarcely amounted to 200 men[38]. The great loss of the French in killed and wounded was caused by their endeavours to re-capture the howitzer, which, on the termination of the battle, was surrounded by the dead soldiers who had attempted its rescue. If Slade had pursued them with his cavalry, the French would have had a sad time of it. To remedy this insufficiency the light division was detached in the route of Val de Espinho, to look for the enemy on the side of the passes leading to Coria. On this eventful day the troops showed a great amount of courage in thus attacking the enemy who had six times their number of men. During the following night Massena continued his retreat, and on the 5th of April crossed the frontiers of Spain, having, in various combats, lost a great many men in killed and wounded, and nearly 3,000 prisoners.

From the manner in which our regiments fought in Spain and Portugal, they were rechristened, or, as you would call it, 'nicknamed.' It would, perhaps, interest you if I were to give you the names of a few of these 'nicknamed' regiments, and the reason why, as well as I can, that they were so called. The 28th regiment distinguished itself greatly at the battle of Barossa, in the south of Spain, and they have a distinction which, perhaps, no other regiment in the world enjoys, that is, they are allowed to wear a badge on the back as well as on the front of their shakos. If you ever chance to meet one of the 28th regiment now, you will find him thus doubly decorated. We always used to say they were decorated 'fore and aft.' They did not obtain this distinction in the Peninsula, but for their conduct at Alexandria, in Egypt, under the command of Sir Edward Paget. They were nicknamed 'The Slashers,' and acquired the emblem of double decoration. The

---

36 Major General Sir Charles Colville.

37 These figures are difficult to ascertain as the French returns in Oman only show losses of 760 in total; however it is clear that these returns are very far from complete.

38 Allied losses at Sabugal were 162 in total of killed, wounded and missing.

57th regiment (now in Manchester I believe, but I scarcely think there will be any of the men in it there were at that time), for their gallant conduct at the battle of Albuera, in Spain, where only one officer was left standing out of twenty-four, and 168 privates out of 584[39], bear the honourable distinction of the 'Diehards,' which is a title the 27th are as justly entitled to for their bravery at Waterloo[40]. The 87th regiment, for their capture of the French eagle at Barossa[41], (a task of no easy performance, as the French, when they were hard pressed, unscrewed their eagles and pocketed them, throwing away the banner-staff and bit of showy silk as a ruse de guerre for the retardment [sic] of the 'Johnny Raws,' as the French used to call us in the English service, are termed, in the true fashion of the Emerald Islanders, 'Sure an aren't they the aigle-ketchers.' They were christened this by an Irish regiment, and were known ever afterwards as 'The aigle-ketchers.' The Royal Regiment being the oldest regiment in any European service – they were enrolled in the year 1633 – were called the 'Pontius Pilate's Guards.' The Queen's regiment was called 'Kirke's Lambs' because they had the Agnus Dei on their appointments[42]. The 89th were christened 'The Yorickers'[43]. The 50th regiment have black facings, and on that account were called 'The Dirty-Half [Hundred] Regiment.' Some regiments are named after the place they were raised at, such as the 88th, having been raised at Connaught, and the 27th in Enniskillen, are called 'The Connaught Rangers' and 'The Enniskilleners.' Other regiments are distinguished by the colour of their facings, that of their uniform, or that of their horses; for instance, 'The Pompadours', 'The Buffs', 'The Oxford Blues', 'The Scots Greys'[44], etc.

Even divisions of the army have been 'nicknamed' according to peculiar circumstances. The 3rd division having had a large share of the hard knocks,

---

39 Oman states the 57th Regiment as having 31 officers and 616 men at Albuera and they suffered 2 officers and 87 men killed, 21 officers and 318 men wounded and no missing. This means that they suffered 428 casualties, leaving only 188 unharmed, of which 8 were officers.

40 The 27th were not given this name after Waterloo, but Smithie indicates that they deserved it.

41 Sergeant Masterson of 87th captured the eagle of the 8eme Ligne Regiment.

42 Agnus Dei – Latin: Lamb of God.

43 I have been unable to establish this nickname to the 89th or any other regiment. In fact the 89th were usually nicknamed 'Blayney's Bloodhounds'.

44 The Pompadours – 56th Foot (Rose pink cuffs & collars)

The Buffs – 3rd Foot (Buff cuffs & collars)

The Oxford Blues – Horse Guards (Earl of Oxford's livery was blue)

The Scots Greys – The 2nd Dragoons (they rode grey horses)

and other pleasantries of warfare, were entitled 'The Fighting Division.' The 4th division were called 'The Enthusiasts' by Lord Wellington himself in his despatch respecting the battle of Pamplona. The light division consisting of the matchless soldiers of the 43rd and 52nd regiments and the 95th rifles, were, on account of their being constantly employed and forming the advance and rear guards of the army called 'The War Brigade,' and another division were called 'The Immortals'[45]. Regiments in the French army have their 'nicknames' as well as ours, and I freely admit with as just a title to them as any of the English regiments, for that nation is truly a nation of warriors; they are born soldiers, and would almost be unconquerable if they possessed the same spirit of endurance and coolness of the English. The 4th demi-brigade and the 37th demi-brigade of the army of Italy were styled 'The Impetuous,' and sometimes 'The Terrible.' The column of grenadiers that formed the advanced guard of the army of the Western Pyrenees, was surnamed 'The Infernals.' The chasseurs of the Imperial guard were styled 'The Invincibles,' and the 45th of the line 'The Immortals.' The same practice prevails in nearly every service in Europe, and the entire service of nations have likewise their 'nicknames' Thus the English soldiers call those of France 'The Johnny Crapauds,' while the French designated we fellows in red jackets – who never knew when we were beaten –'Les Goddams'[46], and sometimes 'The Johnny Raws.' Our troops in the Peninsular war termed the Spaniards Los Carajos[47], from their terrible swearing, and their no less terrible runnings [sic] away.

These are as many of the 'nicknames' as I can remember at present, but there were a great many others who were 'nicknamed' like those I have mentioned, from their having accomplished some daring feat or other.

The next affair of importance that occurred after we crossed the frontiers of Spain was at Badajoz. We were under the command of Sir William Beresford, and on the 23rd of March our advanced guard, consisting of 2,000 cavalry and a brigade of infantry, under Colonel Colbourne, came up with the enemy, who, having heard that we were coming, were beginning to evacuate Campo Maior[48].

---

45 The Immortals were the 76th Foot, not a nickname for a division.
46 A French term for the English since the Hundred Years War.
47 A particularly strong expletive.
48 The Action of Campo Maior actually occurred on 25 March 1811. The French cavalry of Lautour Maubourg was tasked with escorting a convoy of siege artillery to Badajoz. The Allied cavalry overran the French cavalry but then went on an uncontrolled dash right up to the glacis of the fortress before being pushed back. The siege artillery, although at the total mercy of the allies was retaken by the

Their retreat was covered by a strong detachment of French hussars, but these being insufficient to beat off their pursuers four regiments of dragoons advanced to their support[49]. Our 13th light dragoons and a French regiment, facing each other, then charged with loose reins, and the shock was so tremendous that many on both sides were thrown from their horses. They pierced through on both sides, then, reforming, charged again, when the 13th galloped forwards, cut down the gunners that were conducting the battering train, and went on until they reached the French column of march, and took from them their goods, stores, and ammunition. But they could, not hold possession of their booty, for the heavy cavalry were not in a position to support them. Some of them formed in front of the French column and returned by cutting their way through, whilst others, who seemed to have gone mad with the excitement, kept up a hand to hand conflict to the very gates of Badajoz, and the consequence was that a great many of them were taken prisoners. This heroic act on the part of the 13th dragoons was greatly admired throughout the army; but Wellington severely reprimanded them for their rashness. When we got possession of Campo Maior, we erected a bridge at the fordable points, made of tressles, but in the course of the night it was carried away by a sudden rising of the river. We were in a 'mess' but it was contrived to make a raft, or temporary bridge of the pontoons and casks we had collected from the surrounding villages; this acted very well for the infantry to pass over, but for the cavalry and artillery another one had to be constructed of Spanish boats; by this means our army crossed the river and took up a position on the left bank. A squadron of the 13th light dragoons was here surprised and captured by a force of French cavalry, about 500 strong, with about 3,500 infantry. General Beresford next advanced to Olivenza. He had with him a division of Portuguese and a battering train, and it was his intention to reduce the place. He arrived there on the 12th and commenced active operations. After two days' firing a breach was made in the wall, and, on the morning of the third day, the governor surrendered the place to save further destruction[50]. On the 16th the 10th Light Dragoons made a 'sally' on two French regiments of hussars, who had been collecting supplies (of which they had already got a great quantity)

French infantry and arrived safely at its destination. This action is used to typify the gung ho attitude of the British cavalry; simply charging at everything.

49   The troops under Brigadier Long engaged were 13th Light Dragoons and 1st & 7th Portuguese cavalry. The French cavalry consisted of 2nd & 10th Hussars and 26th Dragoons. The Royals were not involved in this engagement.

50   Olivenza was captured on 15 April 1811.

and succeeded in capturing a portion of the plunder and killing 300 of them, besides taking many prisoners. Active preparations were now commenced to take Badajoz by storm, but a very sudden and unexpected rising of the river again took away the bridges we had made. You will have an idea of the suddenness with which it rose when I tell you that it only took about 12 hours to rise 9ft. Soult raised the siege of Badajoz[51], and the operations were transferred to Ciudad Rodrigo.

On the 2nd of May our army crossed the River Agueda, at Ciudad Rodrigo, and prepared for battle. The ground chosen for the contest was at Fuentes d'Onoro, one of the most beautiful villages that I ever saw in my life, in fact I could not describe it if I were to attempt; it certainly was too much like a paradise to be wrecked and ruined by the bloody and horrible business that was about to be transacted in its neighbourhood. On the evening of the 3rd the French General Loison, formed his 6th corps on the right bank of the River Agueda, apparently with the intention of forcing our centre. General [Alexander] Campbell was in command of the 6th Division, and he was posted on the bridge near Almeida.

Sir William Erskine commanded the 5th; while the principal part of the army, consisting of the 1st, 3rd, and 7th Divisions were concentrated on Fuentes d'Onoro, behind the village, ready to meet the enemy at whatever point they attacked. Lieut. Col. Williams[52] commanded the force which occupied the village, consisting of the 1st and 3rd Divisions. General Slade commanded our regiment the 1st Royal Dragoons and just before the battle commenced he said, 'Now, Royals, you will have five to one, and if you fight well today you shall have plenty of good wine,' for he knew we liked it. We gave him a cheer, and he went away looking quite satisfied that we should all do our best when the time came. Well, as I said before, the French commander (Massena) made the attempt to pierce our centre, but in this he failed and was forced to retire. He however made play for attacking some of the weaker points in our line. At daylight, on the 5th, two columns of infantry and a body of cavalry under General Junot, attacked our advanced guard and drove it in, and so the Light Division, with cavalry, went to their assistance, when the French cavalry made a furious charge; but though it was a most tremendous shock the Light Brigade unflinchingly maintained their ground, and when they got warmed to their work they went at the French as furiously as they had been attacked; and although the French 'Johnnys' were a good deal stronger in point of numbers, they were forced to retreat in great

---

51 Smithie means that Soult's advance caused Marshal Beresford to raise the siege of Badajoz.
52 Lt. Colonel William Williams 5/60th.

disorder. In the meantime the enemy was gaining ground in the wood, near the village of Poco Velho, and appeared to be massing a great portion of his cavalry and infantry in that direction. The 7th Division was then ordered to take possession of the high ground behind the Turon [rivulet] and the Light Division were ordered to form a reserve in rear of the left of the 1st Division. It appears the enemy thought this movement was a general retreat, and pressed on thinking they had already gained the victory. At one time they had cut off and surrounded with their cavalry Captain Ramsay's battery of horse artillery. In a book I have read ('The Life and Times of Wellington') it says, describing this part of the battle: 'In a moment great confusion and tumult, with sparkling of blades and flashing of pistols in the locality where the gallant band stood, was observed, when they raised a true English cheer, the mass was rent asunder, and Ramsay burst forth sword in hand at the head of his battery; his horses almost breathing fire stretched across the plain, the guns bounding behind them like things of no weight, and the mounted gunners following close with heads bent low and pointed weapons, in desperate array. They had broken their way through the astonished squadrons of the enemy, and brought off the battery. At the same moment Captain Brotherton advanced to their relief with a squadron of the 14th dragoons, and checked the head of the pursuing troops. But the storm of battle throughout the whole day was at Fuentes d'Onoro, for there the principal effort of the enemy was directed. General Drouet made a desperate attack on the village, which was as desperately defended by the 71st, 79th, and 24th British regiments. Their infantry, cavalry, and artillery were all brought to bear, and at 9 o'clock in the morning the signal was given, and Montbrun ordered a charge of the whole French cavalry[53]. When it came to cavalrymen against cavalrymen you may be sure there was some hot and murderous work. Our regiment came face to face with a whole French regiment of hussars. We charged them, but nearly all in the first rank on both sides, men and horses were thrown violently to the ground, and our horses rode over them. We rode through each other, cutting our way, and then, wheeling round, we charged and fought our way back again. I have to tell you of the luckiest escape that I ever had in my life, and it occurred in connection with this charge. The horse I rode was a very spirited one – it was a splendid charger – but

---

53 Montbrun's cavalry drove Wellington's right wing back and there was some fighting between the opposing cavalry at squadron level. Two squadrons under Lt. Colonel Clifton charged the French cavalry taking prisoner a sergeant and 24 men but also releasing a party of the 3rd Foot Guards. This presumably the combat that Smithie describes. The Royals lost 4 men killed and one officer and 36 men wounded with 18 horses killed and another 52 wounded, at Fuentes d'Onoro.

sometimes it had rather more mettle than I liked. As soon as we had cut through them the second time – and though many of our men had fallen, I had got through safely – my horse placed the 'bit' some way in its mouth so that I had no control over it, and turning round dashed in amongst the French cavalry. I began to feel sure that it was certain death for me, but as I was amongst them cutting my way, my horse rearing and plunging madly, and knocking over everything that came in its way, I had to make the best of it. When I got through them it turned again as our regiment had done before, and took me safely through. I never could imagine how it was I got out alive, for although my clothing and knapsack were cut through almost to rags I escaped without a scratch. When I came up with our regiment, which had retired from the fight, the horses were falling dead on all sides, though they were not wounded; and some of the men fainted from sheer exhaustion. As we were going along the road poor Corporal Gibbs, who had been wounded in the fray, could hold up no longer, and he fell from his horse into the ditch, and implored us either to shoot him or to fill him up to smother him from his sufferings. Well, none of us liked to shoot him, and the doctors said it would be impossible for him to survive his wounds, so a few of us dismounted, and after shaking hands with the poor fellow we made a grave with our swords and buried him alive. There was scarcely a man in the whole regiment but what shed tears over him, for he was a jolly sort of fellow, and always a great favourite with us. As soon as the veterinary surgeons could be brought to look at the horses that were dying and dead they made an examination. I saw them open the first, and it was a most awful sight. They declared that the animals' strength had been so severely taxed that the very fat in their insides had become softened and was even melting, and it was from this they were dying. We were not called out any more that day as our horses were not fit to mount. I may as well mention that in the earlier part of the fight I was struck on the belt by a spent ball and very severely hurt; I was examined by the doctor who found my breast quite blackened by the force of the blow; but after being attended to and the wound dressed, I returned to the field and joined my regiment. The battle lasted until evening and ended in the French being put to the rout. The loss of the British was nearly 2,000 in killed, wounded, and taken prisoners; and the French lost 5,000 in killed and prisoners, besides which there were between 3,000 and 4,000 wounded[54].

The next engagement I took part in was at Salamanca, but our regiment acted

---

54 Smithie greatly exaggerates the French losses. Oman states the losses at Fuentes d'Onoro as: Allied, 2,063 killed, wounded and missing; French, 2,844 killed, wounded and prisoners.

as a kind of reserve at the battle of Albuera[55]. I will just mention a few particulars about this battle, because it was about one of the bloodiest that we ever fought in the Peninsula. The leading regiment, the 29th, had no sooner reached the heights than it was exposed to a murderous fire of musketry and artillery, which spread destruction throughout its ranks. But they went on and on, the men being knocked down like so many skittles, until they came to a steep gully, and here they were forced to halt and open fire, as they could not reach the enemy to bayonet them. The 57th regiment fought desperately, but suffered very severely; for out of about 570 privates, 400 of them were slain; and only one officer was left standing out of twenty-four[56]. I believe the 48th and 29th Regiments suffered still more[57]. The Fusiliers had a desperate fight, and only won the day with their splendid charges of the bayonet. The French were not equal to English soldiers in the use of the bayonet, and did not like the idea of having cold steel run through them. In a book which was afterwards written, it said, commenting on the battle: 'Such a gallant line, issuing from the midst of the smoke, and rapidly separating itself from the confused multitude, startled the enemy's heavy masses, which were increasing and pressing onward as to an assured victory; they wavered, hesitated, and then, vomiting forth a storm of fire, hastily endeavoured to enlarge their front, while a fearful discharge of grape from all their artillery whistled through the British ranks. Myers was killed[58]; Cole[59] (with nearly all his Staff) and three colonels were wounded; and the Fusilier battalions, struck with the iron tempest, reeled and staggered like sinking ships. Suddenly and sternly recovering, they closed on their terrible enemies, and then was seen with what a strength and majesty English soldiers fight. In vain did Soult by voice and gesture animate his Frenchmen; in vain did the hardiest veterans, extricating themselves from the crowded columns, sacrifice their lives to gain time for the mass to open out on so fair a field; in vain did the mass itself bear, and fiercely striving, fire indiscriminately on friends and foes; while their horsemen, hovering on to the flank, threatened to charge the advancing line. Nothing could stop that astonishing infantry. No sudden burst of undisciplined valour; no nervous enthusiasm weakened the stability of order; their

---

55   On 11 June the regiment marched south through Castelo Branco and Vila Velha de Rodao to Nisa; arriving at Portalegre on 23 June. However, they were no nearer the battlefield of Albuera on 16 May. Smithie stretches the truth in stating that the Royals formed 'a kind of reserve'.

56   See note 39.

57   These two regiments suffered similar levels of casualties to the 57th.

58   Lt. Colonel Sir William Myers commanded the 7th Fusiliers at Albuera and was killed.

59   Major General Sir Lowry Cole was slightly wounded at Albuera.

flashing eyes were bent on the dark columns in their front; their measured tread shook the ground; their dreadful volleys swept away the head of every formation; their deafening shouts overpowered the dissonant cries that broke from all parts of the tumultuous crowd, as foot by foot, and with horrid carnage, it was driven by the incessant vigour of the attack to the farthest edge of the hill. In vain did the French reserves, joining with the struggling multitude, endeavour to sustain the fight; their efforts only increased their irremedial confusion, and the mighty mass, giving way like a loosened cliff, went headlong down the ascent. The rain flowed after in streams, discoloured with blood, and 1,500 unwounded men, the remnant of 6,000 unconquerable soldiers, stood triumphant on the fatal hill'[60]. Those are the grandest words I ever heard used to describe a battle. The loss on each side in this fierce and bloody battle was great. Our loss amounted to 7,000, of whom all were English, excepting 2,500 Spaniards, Germans, and Portuguese. The French have admitted their loss to be betwixt 8,000 and 9,000[61]. They then retreated.

The next engagements that took place were at Ciudad Rodrigo and Badajoz[62], which were stormed; but our cavalry were not brought into force, as the fighting was done by the artillery and storming parties. Massena had got his nose cut off by one of our soldiers in an affair that had taken place a day or two previously, and in which he had lost 5,000 men; and about the same time Buonaparte recalled him, and placed the command of his army into the hands of Marshal Marmont. It was said that Buonaparte had become disgusted because Massena had not 'driven us into the sea,' and he ordered him to repair to his presence in the French capital[63]. When Buonaparte saw him he said, 'Marshal, where have you left your nose?' to which he replied, 'With my comrades, sire,' 'And where may you have left your comrades, then?' 'I left them along with my nose,' said he, the emperor evidently being pleased with his wit. It is rather singular too that Marshal Marmont was also wounded; in the very next engagement, at Salamanca, he got his arm taken off by a cannon ball[64]. On the occurrence of this accident Marshal Bonet assumed

---

60 A quote from William Napier's History of the Peninsular War published in 1836.

61 Oman states the Allied losses at Albuera as: British 4,159, Portuguese 389, Spanish 1,368; giving a total of 5,916. French losses were around 8,000.

62 Ciudad Rodrigo was stormed on 19 January and Badajoz on 6 April 1812. The Royals were in the vicinity, covering the operations at both sieges, but were not involved.

63 This comment regarding Massena is out of place in the text. Massena was recalled after the defeat at Fuentes d'Onoro. The story of his nose is complete fabrication.

64 The story that Marmont lost an arm was prevalent at this time; he was wounded in the arm by a shell exploding but did keep his arm.

the temporary command in chief of the French forces.

The battle of Salamanca raged with great fury for seven hours, and resulted in a total defeat of the French[65]. The loss had been great on both sides. We had lost 5,600 in killed and wounded, of which 500 British had been killed, 3,000 had been wounded, and about 1,000 taken prisoners; of the Portuguese 338 were killed, 1,648 wounded, and 207 were missing; of the Spaniards only two were killed and four wounded![66] General Marchant was killed, and Generals Beresford, Cotton, Leith, Cole, and Spry[67] were wounded. We captured 7,000 prisoners, two eagles, eleven cannon, and were left in possession of the field, which was covered with the slain and the wounded[68]. There were many instances of valour shown at this battle, but the most conspicuous were those of Captain Brotherton, of the 14th Light Dragoons[69], who, having received a severe wound in his side in a recent skirmish, not being allowed to serve with his regiment in an undress, he joined a Portuguese regiment and was wounded a second time in assaulting the Arapiles; Captain Mackie of the 88th[70], after heading his regiment throughout their advance against the foe, joined our regiment and went through every charge; and a man who was shot through the middle, having lost his shoes in passing the marshy stream, refused to quit the fight, and limped under fire in rear of his regiment, with blood streaming from his wound.

But the most extraordinary thing of this character took place at the battle of Albuera, which I have before described. At that battle, Ensign Thomas, of the Buffs, was ordered to surrender the colours he carried, and refusing to comply he was cloven in two[71]. The colour staff was broken in two in the hand of Ensign Walsh, and, falling wounded on the field in the agonies of death, the brave youth

---

65 The Royals were not at Salamanca for the battle; they were still serving in the south near Albuera.

66 The casualty returns for Salamanca by Oman show the allies lost 4,762 killed & wounded in total. The British lost 388 killed, 2,267 wounded and 74 missing; the Portuguese 508 killed, 1,035 wounded and 86 missing and the Spanish as Smithie states, 2 killed and 4 wounded. The French loss was around 14,000 including 7,000 prisoners.

67 Brevet Colonel William Spry served with the Portuguese Army, commanding a brigade.

68 The eagles of the 22nd Ligne and 62nd Ligne were captured and 20 cannon (although Wellington's dispatch states 11).

69 Captain Brotherton is not recorded as having received a previous wound, but was slightly wounded at Salamanca.

70 It is recorded that Captain Mackie joined the cavalry in their charges and returned to his regiment with only the hilt of his sword left and covered in blood.

71 Ensign Edward Thomas 3rd Foot was killed trying to protect the colours.

tore the colours from his broken staff and thrust them in his bosom, where they were found dyed in blood after his death.

Lieutenant Latham, who carried the colours of the Buffs, was attacked by several French hussars, when one of them seized hold of the staff, at the same time rising in his stirrups and aiming a blow at the lieutenant's head, which cut off his nose and one side of the face. Still he retained his hold of the colour, and being ordered to give it up, he exclaimed, 'I will surrender it only with my life.' A second stroke from the Frenchman severed his left hand and arm, when, throwing away his sword, he seized the colour with his right hand, and continuing to struggle with his cowardly foe, he was pierced by the spears of some Polish lancers who were coming up to their assistance. The enemy being driven off by Houghton's brigade, Latham's last effort was to tear the flag from the staff and thrust it partly into the breast of his jacket. After the battle, the colour being found where he had placed it, it was sent to the head quarters of the Buffs; but life being supposed to be extinct in the body of its brave defender, he was left on the field. Shortly recovering his senses be crawled on his knees and his right hand to the river Albuera to slake his fevered and parched throat, and there he was found by one of the orderlies of the regiment; he was conveyed to the convent, where the stump of his shattered arm was amputated, and in the course of time he was restored to health.

For this noble devotion he was promoted to a company in the Canadian Fencible Infantry; but afterwards, on a vacancy occurring, he rejoined his own regiment. He was presented with a gold medal for this act by the officers of the regiment[72]. Sir William Beresford was attacked by a Polish lancer, and throwing aside the weapon of his adversary, he seized hold of him, threw him upon the ground, and offered him quarter, but as he refused to yield, Sir William ordered his orderly to despatch him, which he did.

Wellington himself was struck with a bullet at the battle of Salamanca[73], and he had many narrow escapes in other engagements. At the battle of Assaye – where he fought in the East Indian war – while crossing the River Kaitna, the head of an orderly who was close by his side, was struck off by a cannon ball; he had two horses killed under him; and the tree under which he stood was pierced with

---

72 Smithie has mixed the stories of Ensign Walsh and Lieutenant Latham together. Walsh was in charge of the colours but the colours were taken from him by Latham just before he surrendered. Latham did experience all that Smithie describes and incredibly survived. Initially Walsh was credited with saving the colour but on his return from captivity he readily gave full credit to Latham.

73 He was hit on the thigh by a spent bullet.

balls. At the battle of Talavera two balls cut through his coat; a spent ball struck him on the shoulder[74]; a branch of a tree under which he stood was struck off just above his head by a cannon ball; and while reconnoitering the enemy at the Casa de Salinas he was nearly captured. During the movements of the English and French armies preceding the battle of Salamanca, the Duke, while observing the enemy's movements, was surrounded by the French cavalry, and it was with great difficulty that he and his staff could extricate themselves[75]. At the battle of Vitoria, he passed unharmed through the fire of the French centre which consisted of 80 pieces of artillery. In the battle of Sorauren, July 28th, 1813, while sat in observation on the heights, within close musket range, a ball, which struck the breast-plate of the Marquis of Westminster's sword[76], and threw him from his horse, grazed Lord Wellington.

On the same evening he was so nearly captured by a detachment of the enemy, that it was almost a miracle he escaped from the volley of shot that poured on them while they galloped away. At the battle of Orthes he was struck by a spent ball. At the battle of Waterloo, the elm tree which was in the centre of the British line, and under which he took post during part of the battle, was pierced with balls. He was also threatened with assassination twice whilst in France, and Bonaparte bequeathed a legacy of 10,000 francs to the would be murderer.

But to return to my story. Whilst the battle of Salamanca was being fought, the inhabitants watched from the high grounds above the city the various changes of the battle, with painful anxiety, and when the French had been totally put to the rout, and the allies entered the town, they were received with every manifestation of joy. They sent mules and cars laden with refreshment to the field of battle; they took especial care of the wounded; and every exertion was made to relieve their sufferings. Spanish girls came out and assisted such of the wounded who could walk, by supporting them, carrying their knapsacks and muskets to the hospital. As I was passing over to my quarters, after the din had ceased, my captain, Lord Montagu, came up to me with a beautiful gold-hilted sword which he had picked up on the field. He said he would make me a present of it (at the same time handing it to me) on condition that if the owner was found that I would deliver it up to him. I thanked his lordship for it, and promised to do as he had said. He had not left me more than five minutes when a little drummer-boy who was passing saw the sword I held in my hand, and instantly cried out, 'That's my captain's

---

74 He was bruised by a spent bullet.

75 A false rumour.

76 This would be Worcester aide de camp to Wellington not Westminster. An error by Smithie.

sword.' I went with him to his tent, where I found the captain, who was having his wounds dressed. He told me he was Captain Hardy, of the Foot Guards, and that he would handsomely reward me for restoring his sword, which you may be sure was a very valuable one. I did not get nor expect any reward, and do not remember ever seeing him again[77]. High mass was said in the cathedral, at which Wellington attended by invitation, and it was conducted with great ceremony on account of the victory which had been gained. The enemy retreated in great haste from Salamanca, in the direction of Madrid. We followed up expecting they would make a stand at that place, but we were agreeably disappointed, for on they rushed, and did not concentrate their forces until they reached Burgos.

It was on the 12th day of August[78], 1812, when we made our triumphal entry into Madrid. It was a day of jubilee – all business was suspended – the inhabitants came out in great crowds, holding branches of laurel in their hands – and welcomed us at the gates with tears of joy, the waving of handkerchiefs, and also showered flowers upon us to evince their joy and gratitude. The females embraced every soldier that came in their path, and insisted on taking wine with him at almost every corner. The inhabitants crowded round Wellington, hung on his stirrups, touched his clothes, and some fell upon the ground and blessed him aloud as the friend of Spain[79].

Wellington lost no time in reconnoitering the Retiro palace, which the French had strongly fortified, and was garrisoned by 2,500 men on the east of Madrid. It contained about 20,000 stand of arms, 180 pieces of brass cannon, eight field guns, and an immense quantity of trenching tools and stores. The eagles of the 13th and 57th French regiments were deposited there. By the evening of the 13th the place was completely invested; and on the morning of the 14th, while arrangements were being made for the attack, the commander surrendered[80]. On the evening of the 13th, Don Carlos de Espana was proclaimed governor of Madrid, amidst the cheers of an immense throng. All the population seemed to turn out into the streets and squares, and the scene was truly grand. The Duke

---

77 Unfortunately this passage regarding Salamanca would appear to be a tall tale. The regiment was not at Salamanca, but near Albuera at this time; Montagu had already resigned his commission in the summer of 1811 and left the Army and there was no Captain Hardy in the Foot Guards.

78 They actually marched into Madrid on 13 August.

79 The Royals were still in the south of the country with General Hill and therefore did not enter Madrid with Wellington.

80 The Retiro was captured on 14 August with 20,000 muskets and 180 cannon in store. However the eagles captured were actually the 13th Dragoons and the 51st Ligne.

rode through the town, attended by a great number of English noblemen and officers of his staff, when the Spanish nobles and church dignitaries came out to meet him and present him with the keys. We could scarce hear anything but the cheers of the populace, who were exclaiming at the very top of their voices, 'Long live the great Duke of Rodrigo, the illustrious conqueror.' The Spanish ladies, elegantly dressed, not only threw laurels and flowers, but spread shawls and veils of the finest texture for him to walk over. When he attempted to alight at the palace, where he was to reside, ladies of the first rank embraced and kissed him, and even every person they took to be him, so that it was some time before he and his generals could get housed. We had no trouble in getting billets; we were welcome anywhere. I remember that I and a comrade or two were seeking a place to rest for the night, and when passing a large house a gentleman got hold of my arm, and called of his wife and daughters to fetch the others in. We happened to be looking out our quarters, and it was luckily we got such comfortable lodgings, for we had not slept on a bed for more than 12 months, and we found it a deal more pleasant than lying on the hard ground with nothing but the sky and a rug over us. We spent a very pleasant evening; there were fruits and wine in abundance, and the daughters played and sung beautifully for us. They seemed very sorry to part with us[81]. The Duke attended a Spanish bull fight, which had been got up on a scale of unusual splendour in honour of his presence. At this fight it was estimated that there were 12,000 persons present, who repeatedly cheered him.

The allies evacuated Madrid[82], and pursued the French to Burgos, a strongly fortified town. Wellington determined to lay siege to it; but after battering away at it for thirty days, and apparently without any effect, he ordered a retreat of the whole army, which was made accordingly. We fell back on Salamanca through Madrid, and here we took up our quarters for the winter[83].

The campaign of 1813 commenced in the beginning of March, after the most severe of the winter had been experienced. The position of the hostile armies was as follows: the main body of the British and Portuguese were quartered in cantonments along the northern frontiers of Portugal to Lamego. The Second

---

81   This passage must refer to the period of October 1812 when Hill's Corps including the Royals moved up to Madrid and its environs.

82   The allies did not leave Madrid at this time; only half of the army moved to Burgos.

83   This retreat, which commenced for the Royals on 27 October, continued all the way to the Portuguese border, the troops suffering greatly from fatigue and starvation, the commissary having retreated earlier. The regiment wintered at Zibreira (16 miles from Alcantara).

James Smithies in later life wearing his Peninsula and Waterloo medals.

The gravestone of James Smithies, his wife Ann and two children James and Ann.

1st Royal Dragoons re-enactment group.

Trooper, 1st (Royal) Dragoons 1815 by Bob Marrion

Division, under Hill, and a division of Spaniards, were in Upper Estremadura. The army of Gallicia, under General Giron, occupied the frontier of that province. The French force in Spain was at that time 170,000 efficient men; and of these 70,000 constituted the armies of Portugal, the centre and the south. The army of Portugal, under Reille, occupied the country between the rivers Esla and Carrion. That of the centre was under Marshal Drouet, and stationed at Segovia and Valladolid; and that on the south under Marshal Gazan, occupied Madrid, Salamanca, Toro, and Zamora.

The whole of these were under the command of Joseph Bonaparte (who was brother to Napoleon Bonaparte), assisted by Marshal Jourdan, his major-general. The French, during the winter, fortified their naturally strong position on the northern bank of the river Douro at every assailable point, by works and entrenchments. They also apprehended that Wellington's plan was to make an attack on Madrid, and made their dispositions accordingly to counteract this movement. But the real fact was that the duke had another scheme, which was that the left wing of the allies should move across the Douro, within the Portuguese frontier, marching it up the right or northern bank of that river, and then crossing the Esla, to unite it with the Gallician forces under General Giron; whilst the centre and right wing, advancing from the river Agueda by Salamanca, forced the passage of the Tormes, and drove the French from the line of the Douro, and intercepting the whole line of communication. To put this masterly plan into execution, he prepared means of transport at Lamego and other places. On the 15th of May he threw five divisions of infantry and two brigades of cavalry, in all about 40,000 men, under General Graham, across the Douro, with orders to march through the province of Tras-os-Montes, on Zamora. When Graham was supposed to be sufficiently advanced on May 22nd, the main body of the army, about 28,000 men, advanced in two lines towards the river Tormes: the right consisting of the 2nd Division of Murillo's corps, under Hill, from Upper Estremadura on Alba de Tormes, a town on the Tormes, a little south of Salamanca; and the left, consisting of two of our divisions of infantry, some Portuguese divisions of infantry, and five brigades of cavalry, by Matilla upon Salamanca, under the command of Wellington in person. The whole army was in high spirits, and went merrily on the march. Wellington himself, as we were leaving the boundary of Portugal and entering Spain again, got up in his stirrups and cried 'Farewell Portugal' and the soldiers cheered as they went along, While the allies were preparing to march, Joseph Bonaparte put the army of the centre in motion, and followed by those of the south and Portugal, retreated slowly to the river Ebro.

The appearance of the French army on the march was very picturesque, indeed. It was crowded in its march, and fanciful both in the character of its equipment, and the variety of its costume. Very few of the regiments were dressed alike the line and light infantry excepted. The horse artillery wore uniform of light blue, braided with black lace. The heavy cavalry wore green coats with brass helmets. The chasseurs and hussars, who were mounted on slight, but active horses, were showily and variously equipped. The gendarmerie, the picked men of the whole cavalry, had long blue frocks, with cocked hats and buff belts, whilst a number of dragoons, who, it appeared, were selected for their superior size and general appearance, wore bearskin caps. Each regiment of the line had its company of grenadiers and voltigeurs and even the light regiments had a company of the former. The appearance of the whole force was soldierly and imposing; the cavalry was indeed superb; and the artillery was most complete; and, better still, their horses were in good condition. Both armies, then, were in a state of great efficiency, for to both the commanding officers had given their undivided attention; and yet they looked very dissimilar. With our army everything was simple, compact, and limited; while the French were sadly encumbered with useless equipages and accumulated plunder. Those of the Spanish nobles who had acknowledged Joseph Bonaparte the usurper, now accompanied his retreat; state functionaries, in court dresses and rich embroidery, were intermixed with the troops; while nuns from Castile and ladies from Andalusia, mounted on horseback, deserted castle and convent to follow the fortunes of the soldiers. Our centre and right effected their junction on the 25th of May, at Alba de Tormes, and so rapid had been our march that the French in Salamanca, consisting of 3,000 infantry and 400 cavalry, were nearly surprised, and in their retreat by the defiles of Aldealengua, our regiment (under command of General Fane) pursued them, and besides killing more than 200 of them, and taking many prisoners[84], we got seven guns with their tumbrils[85].

By the way, I may as well tell you that General Slade had been removed from the command of the 'First Royals,' our regiment, and had been superseded by General Fane[86]. He was a clever officer, and never a better ever handled a sword. It was said – I believe it to be true too – that Mrs. Clarke, well known

---

84   General Villatte left Salamanca in the direction of Aldealengua, but was intercepted by the Royals. The right squadron commanded by Lt. Colonel Clifton charged and made 143 prisoners and 7 tumbrils, but no cannon. It is unlikely that anywhere near as many as 200 were killed.

85   Tumbrils: waggons for spare ammunition.

86   Major General Henry Fane.

in connection with the Duke of York, had recommended Fane to be made a general; and he deserved his promotion, for he had acted bravely in many a hard fought battle. I said at the time, that if Mrs. Clarke had really been the cause of General Fane's promotion, she ought to be made a Field-Marshal! It created quite a 'stir' amongst our men, and an enterprising toy seller manufactured a lot of snuff and tobacco boxes with the likeness of the Duke of York on one side, and Mrs. Clarke on the other, and he had an enormous trade in them.

The right and centre then advanced the first towards Zamora, where it was proposed to throw over the bridge; the right was pushed towards Toro, and covered the communication with Ciudad Rodrigo. The army being now halted between the rivers Tormes and Douro, Wellington transferred the command to Lord Hill, for the time, whilst he (the Duke) went to see how his combinations on the Esla were going on. On the 30th May he passed the Miranda do Douro – which here runs foaming between two rocks about 500 feet high – by means of a hammock or cradle, slung by rings attached to a rope stretched across from precipice to precipice. On the day following he reached Carbajales [de Alba] and assumed the direction of the left wing, which was then on the Esla, and in communication with the Galician army. Preparations were now made for passing the Esla. As the opposite banks were watched by pickets of cavalry and infantry, at daybreak on the 31st, a brigade of hussars (with a foot soldier of the 51st and the Brunswick Oels, holding chin-deep to the stirrup of every horseman) effected the passage with very trifling loss. We found this to be a very good way of sending foot soldiers across a river, and when they landed they captured one of the enemy's pickets. It was in this way that the great line of the Douro was turned, and the defensive works of the enemy rendered useless. They immediately destroyed the bridges of Zamora and Toro, and abandoned their posts in haste. We entered Zamora on the 1st of June, and Toro on the day following. Threatened by the advance, the enemy retreated with precipitation; but their rear guard was overtaken by Colonel Grant's hussars. The French horsemen retreated across the bridge, and formed themselves into two lines, and awaited the British charge; but our 10th and 18th regiments, dashing forwards, broke their lines, took above 200 prisoners, and pursued the fugitives until they took shelter under their guns. This affair afforded a proof of the indifference with which a people familiarised to danger, regard events which in ordinary times are looked upon with horror[87]. The Spaniards now were so accustomed to sights of war that though the fighting

---

87 The Combat of Morales occurred on 2 June. Two officers and 208 men of the French 16th Dragoons were captured in this affair.

had almost been in the streets of Morales, within ten minutes after the firing had ceased, the women were spinning at their doors, and the little children at play.

The rapid advance of our army having placed that of Joseph Bonaparte in a perilous position, as if it remained where it was it would be cut off from the army of Portugal, and from its line of communication with France, 'Joseph' quitted Madrid in no small hurry, and crossed the river at Puentes [Viejas] and effected a junction with Marshal Reille. They however, retreated and entered Burgos on the 14th, but not considering themselves secure even there, they destroyed the interior of the castle by exploding the defences. It was their intention to have destroyed both the town and castle, but either from hurry or negligence the mines exploded outwards. Many perished in the town; and a column defiling at the time under the castle, 300 of the men were crushed to death in the ruins. After abandoning Burgos the French retreated in the night, and having garrisoned the castle of Pancorbo, standing at a short distance from the rivers, which commands the pass of that name, and the bridge of Miranda de Ebro, they took up a strong position; the army of the south at Miranda, that of the centre at Haro on the left, and that of Portugal on the right ; and thus possessed of the rocks, the long narrow pass, the castle of Pancorbo, they imagined they might safely wait for the reinforcements from Biscay, Navarre, and Aragon. Their army in [of] Portugal was cantoned in divisions as far as Arminon[88], for the purpose of observing the movements in the front. Wellington, though he had crossed the Tormes, Esla, Douro, Carrion, Pisuerga, Arlanzon, and rocks, mountains, and ravines, as if they had been dried and levelled lands, aware of the difficulties of the Pancorbo pass, and the strong positions on the Ebro, instead of forcing the passage of that river in face of an army, determined to effect the purpose by the same manoeuvres he had put into practice at the Douro: of moving on the flank of the enemy and taking the defensive positions in reverse. For this purpose he struck to his left, by the road to Santander, and conducting his men by one of the most difficult routes ever traversed by an army, to the bridges of San Martin [de Mancobo], Rocamonde, and Puente de Arenas, near the source of the river Ebro, his army passed the river on the 14th and 15th. To give you an idea of the difficulty we experienced in travelling, I may just mention it took a hundred men to move a single piece of artillery; we were obliged to dismount one gun and lower it down the precipice by means of ropes. All those passages were much higher up the Ebro than Frias, the highest point the French had thought it necessary to guard. At the same time the Biscayan guerillas occupied all the passes in the mountains

---

88   About 5 miles east of Miranda de Ebro.

which lie between the Ebro and the sea coast. Thus the French were not only obliged to abandon all their defensive positions on the Ebro, but the whole sea coast of Biscay. The allies also gained a new base close by the scene of action. All the military establishments were in consequence removed from Portugal, and the surplus of the army directed to this quarter[89].

On the 16th the allies passing through the rugged and defensible passes, descended on the great road to Bilbao, and continued their march on Vitoria. Marshal Reille, who had been ordered to protect Bilbao, advanced with two divisions in the direction of Orduna, directing Mancune to march with his division from Frias to same point; but on reaching Osuna, he was confronted by General Graham, with the First and Fifth Divisions, who were already in possession of the road to Bilbao. A sharp skirmish ensued, when the sound of battle coming upon them from beyond the mountains, Marshal Reille, suspecting what had happened to Mancune, fell back towards Espejo; and on reaching the spot where the mouths of the valley open on each other, masses of Mancune's Division burst from the hills in all the confusion of defeat, pursued by our Light Division which had been moving in a parallel line with Graham's march. Mancune's Division had sustained a very severe defeat; having crossed the river Aracena, cleared its passes, they had halted on the heights of San Millan[90], to wait for the remainder of the division which was marching with the baggage, when, most unexpectedly, our light division presented itself on a hill directly in front of them.

The ground was not favourable for an attack, the road being steep, narrow, and rugged, overhung with crags and copse wood, and some straggling cottages affording cover to the enemy's voltigeurs. But, undiscouraged by these disadvantages, 'the fighting division,' consisting of the 95th and 52nd, rushed down the hill, and after a sharp fusillade the enemy gave way, closely followed by their assailants; when, on a sudden, the other French brigade, issuing from the pass, appeared on the flank of the assailants. Both sides rushed on to gain the crest of the hill, and both reached the summit together. The 52nd, bringing their flank forward in a run, faced sharply round, and charged with the bayonet. The conflict did not last long; the enemy broke, threw away their knapsacks and arms, and fled with all speed towards Espejo. They lost 400 men in killed and prisoners. Marshal Reille and Mancune effected a junction the same evening, and proceeded in a night march to occupy Subijana do Morillos, on the river Bayas, and about six

---

89 Wellington changed the whole supply route from Lisbon to one from Santander thereby shortening supply lines greatly.

90 This refers to the Action of San Millan which occurred on 18 June 1813.

miles from the Puebla pass, in order to enable the armies of the south and the centre to move safely through the narrow gorge of the Puebla de Arganzan into the valley of the Zadorra, and thus keep open the high road to Bayonne; but while the armies of centre and the south were struggling through the pass, Reille's flank having been turned by the Light Division, and his front assailed by the fourth division, he was driven over the Zadorra on the armies of the south and centre. On the morning of the 19th, the enemy took post about two miles in front of Vitoria; the army of the centre occupying a range of heights in front of the village of Arinez, that of Portugal on the heights of Zuazo. On the 20th, the whole British army, excepting the 6th Division, which was behind escorting the march of the magazines and stores, was concentrated on the right bank of the Bayas. I remember when reading the History of Europe, it said, in speaking of the masterly manner in which the movements of the army had been performed in this march: 'With such accuracy were the marches of all the columns calculated, and with such precision were they carried out by the admirable troops, inured to war and all its fatigues, which Wellington commanded, that everything happened exactly as he had arranged before he set out from Portugal; and the troops all arrived at the stations assigned them, in the prophetic contemplation of their chief, in the neighbourhood of Vitoria, at the very time when the French army, heavily laden and dejected, had accumulated its immense files of chariots and baggage wagons, under the charge of 70,000 men, in the plain in front of that town. No words can do justice to the exquisite beauty of the scenery through which the British troops, especially those on the left wing, passed during this memorable march. The romantic valleys of the mountain region whence the Ebro draws its waters, which at every season excite the admiration of the passing traveller, were at that time singularly enhanced by the exquisite verdure of the opening spring, and the luxuriance of the foliage which in every sheltered nook clothed the mountain sides. War appeared in these sequestered and pastured valleys, not in its rude and bloody garb, but in its most brilliant and attractive costume; the pomp of military music, as the troops wended their way through the valleys, blended with the shepherd's pipe on the hills above; while the numerous columns of horse, foot, and cannon, winding in every direction through the defiles, gave an inexpressible variety and charm to the landscape. Even the common soldiers were not insensible to the beauty of the spectacle thus perpetually placed before their eyes. Often the men rested on their muskets with their arms crossed, gazing on the lovely scenes which lay spread far beneath their feet; and more than once the heads of the columns involuntarily halted to satiate their eyes with a spectacle of beauty, the like of which all felt they might never see again'. We were now at Vitoria, a place which every Englishman has heard of, for there the fate of Napoleon's invasion of the Peninsula was sealed. It was there his army received such a sound thrashing, besides losing nearly all the artillery, baggage, and property it had stolen from the Spanish and Portuguese.

I composed a verse or two while at this place, which was put to a tune and sung a great deal in our regiment, they were as follows:

> When I was an infant, in fancy would say,
> That when older, I would be a soldier,
> Rattles and toys would throw away
> To enlist for a gun or a sabre.
>
> CHORUS
>
> Roll, drums, merrily march away,
> soldiers' glory lives in story;
> His laurels are green when his locks are grey,
> And it's 'Hey for the life of a soldier'
>
> Up, a youngster, then I grew,
> I saw one day a grand review,
> Colours flying, set me dying
> To embark in a life so new.
>
> Who were so merry as we in camp?
> The battle over, we lived in clover Care
> – and our enemies – were forc'd to tramp;
> And this is social order.
> Enlisted to battle, we marched along,
> Courting danger, to fear a stranger,
> The cannons beat time to the trumpets' sound,
> Which made our hearts still braver.
>
> 'Charge!' our gallant captain cried,
> On like lions then we rose,
> Blood and thunder – foes knock under,
> Then, 'Hurrah for victory!'

Then we laugh, we prance, we sing,
Time goes gaily on the wing,
The smiles of beauty sweeten duty,
And each private is a king.

I need scarcely give a detailed account of the battle at Vitoria, as it will perhaps suffice if I give a short description of the place and the result of the engagement. On the evening of the 19th, Vitoria was brilliantly illuminated in honour of the presence of Joseph Bonaparte and his army. On the 20th, Wellington and his officers reconnoitered the enemy's position, and made their disposition for attack, and at daybreak the morning following, the order was given to attack them. In the early part of the fight, Colonel Cadogan, who commanded the Second Division[91] and 71st regiment, was mortally wounded, but before he was taken away his men had won the post they had been striving for. This gallant officer refusing to be taken from the field, was carried to the top of a hill and placed with his back leaning against a tree, that he might see the movements of the army; and, just as the French were beginning to retreat, his spirit took its flight. Our army gained almost every point, and a Spanish peasant informing Wellington that the bridge [of] Tres Puentes was negligently guarded, Kempt's Brigade of the Light Division, crossed, led by the peasant, and halted in a concealed situation. The 15th Hussars, came up in a canter and dashed across the bridge in single file. No other attempt was made to dislodge them, except a few round shot thrown – one of which struck off the peasant's head – and by some French cavalry, who approached but retired. Immediately, Colonel Barnard, with Kempt's riflemen, advanced between the French cavalry and the river, and taking the light troops and artillery in flank, engaged them so closely that the English artillerymen, thinking from their dark uniform they were enemies, fired indiscriminately on them as well as their opponents. Under cover of Barnard's attack, Colville's Brigade of Picton's Division passed the bridge of Mendoza. Sir Thomas Picton was a brave soldier, and was always at the head of his brigade in a battle. A little amusing anecdote is told in connection with his taking of this bridge, which you would perhaps like to hear. While the 3rd (Picton's) Division was waiting to cross the Zadorra, he became impatient to receive orders to advance, and inquired of several aides de camp who came near him from head quarters, whether they had any orders for him. His soldiers were anxiously waiting to advance; he knew the spirit of his men, and had some difficulty restraining it. As the day wore on, and the fight got warmer on the

---

91 This is an error. Cadogan commanded a brigade within the 2nd Division.

right he became furious, and turning to one of his officers, said, 'Damn it, Lord Wellington must have forgotten us.' It was nearly noon; the men were getting discontented, as they had not yet been engaged. Picton's blood was at 'boiling point' and he rode about madly looking in every direction for an aide de camp, until at length one galloped up from Wellington. He was looking for the 7th Division under Lord Dalhousie, which had not yet arrived at its post, having to move over some difficult ground. The aide de camp, riding up at full speed, suddenly checked his horse, and inquired of the general if he had seen Lord Dalhousie. Picton was disappointed; he expected now at least he might move; and in a voice that did not seem any softer for the temper he was in at the time, answered in a sharp tone, 'No, sir, I have not seen his lordship; but have you any orders for me?' 'None,' replied the aide de camp. 'Then, pray, Sir,' said the irritated Picton, 'what orders do you bring!' 'Why', said the aide, 'that as soon as Lord Dalhousie, with the 7th Division, shall commence an attack on the bridge, the 4th Division are to support him.' Picton could not relish the idea of any other division fighting in his front; and, drawing himself up to his full height, said to the astonished aide de camp, in a passionate manner, 'You may tell Lord Wellington from me, sir, that the 3rd Division, under my command, shall, in less than ten minutes, attack the bridge, and carry it, too, and the 4th division may support if they choose.' Having thus expressed his intention, he turned from the aide de camp, put himself at the head of his men, who were quickly in motion towards the bridge, encouraging them with the flattering language, 'Come on, ye rascals; come on, ye fighting villains!' I cannot say whether they were 'rascals,' or not – though I suppose he must be a 'rascal' who will turn soldier, – but they proved themselves to be 'fighting villains,' from the manner in which they carried the bridge, in a very short time. By six p.m., the 52nd had stormed Margarita, and the 87th carried Hermandad; the village of Arinez was taken; and every strong position of the enemy either carried or very much weakened. After six o'clock, the village of Gamarra Menor succumbed to a Spanish brigade under Longa, and though the enemy endeavoured to retake it – as it commanded the road to Bayonne – they were driven back. The enemy could now see that they were defeated on all points, and began a very rapid retreat. We pressed forward, but they retreated so quickly that our infantry could not overtake them. So headlong was their flight that they abandoned all their artillery, ammunition, baggage, and six years plunder of the three armies. To escape with their lives seemed to be their only object. Marshal Gazan, one of their commanding officers, afterwards admitted that their generals, officers, and soldiers, were alike reduced to the clothes upon their backs. Very few of the infantry retained their arms, and many threw away their shakos and pouches to expedite their flight. But quickly as they fled, they took great pains to bear off as many of their wounded as possible, and for this purpose a whole regiment of cavalry was dismounted, and the wounded placed upon the backs of the horses, and were thus carried away. They also carefully endeavoured to conceal their dead, stopping occasionally to collect them and throw them into ditches, where they covered them with bushes. We found many such receptacles, some containing ten bodies, others twenty or more. They had likewise set on fire every village they passed through, and sometimes massacred the inhabitants. According to their account, the enemy lost 8,000 in killed, whilst ours was only 740, of which 500 were English[92]. Our 10th Hussars just entered the town as [Joseph] Bonaparte was hastening out of it. He was pursued by Captain Wyndham[93] and a squadron of hussars, and they fired into his carriage; and Joseph had only time to throw himself on his horse and gallop off, under the protection of a regiment of French dragoons. Just to give you an idea of the amount of booty which we captured, I may say that among the things they left behind them were more than 150 pieces of artillery, nearly 500[94] hundred large caissons containing bombs and ammunition, the colours of the 100th [Ligne] Regiment, an immense amount of military stores, the entire baggage trains and field equipage of the three armies, their military chest containing five and a half million of dollars, and the enormous pillage of the three armies of Joseph during the previous six years. The field of battle, and the roads for miles some in the rear were covered with broken-down waggons, cars, and coaches, some stocked with the choicest wares, others laden with eatables, sacks of flour, casks of brandy, barrels and boxes of dollars and doubloons, wearing apparel, silks, laces, satins, jewellery, paintings, sculpture, books and papers of every description. Whole droves of oxen were roaming on the plain, intermingled with an endless number of sheep, goats, cows, horses, and mules. Joseph Bonaparte's sideboard, larder, cellar, wardrobe, and carriages were amongst the abandoned; as were also French countesses, ladies, actresses, nuns, parrots, poodles, and monkeys. Marshal Jourdan's baton was also picked up by a drummer in the 87th regiment, in that officer's carriage; and so ignorant was the finder of its value, that he sold it to one of the Jew camp followers. Being discovered by accident, it was brought to Wellington; but not before the wily Jew had taken off the gold with which it had

---

92 This is a gross exaggeration of French losses. Oman states that Allied losses were just over 5,000 in total (total Allied killed 840; British 519 killed); the French lost 8,000 which included around 2,000 prisoners.

93 Captain Henry Wyndham 10th Light Dragoons.

94 They actually captured 415 caissons.

been tipped. [Joseph] Bonaparte's own sword was also found on the field. The baggage was promptly rifled by our soldiers, camp followers, and the inhabitants of the surrounding towns and villages. We all seized what we could, I know I got a good share, and quite as much as I could carry[95], we took possession of the military chest and loaded ourselves with money; but the greater part of the spoils fell into the hands of the camp followers. You would have laughed your sides sore, I am sure, if you had seen us masquerading about dressed up in the French officers' clothes we had captured; some even had the state robes and court dresses on whilst thousands of our men had various uniforms, richly embroidered. The camp of every division was soon like a fair we made long benches and sold by auction all the plunder that had fallen to our share. Even it came to selling dollars for they were found to be too heavy to carry in great quantities; I sold as many as eight myself for a guinea in order to get my riches in a smaller compass. The night of the battle, instead of being past in getting rest and food, to prepare ourselves for the pursuit on following day, was passed in looking for plunder. The consequence was Wellington found his army knocked up and incapable of following up the pursuit. Then again, the rain came on and that increased our fatigues, and I will be bound to say that nearly one-half of our army had deserted its colours, and had either left with the intention of plundering or to have a drunken 'spree' with the money which had come so easily into their hands. For this splendid victory, Wellington was created a field-marshal by the British government and Duke of Ciudad Rodrigo by the Spanish government. Wellington now determined to lay siege to St. Sebastian. It so happened that my regiment formed the advanced guard, and on our march we saw much of what I have just described. I remember one incident very particularly. As we were leaving Vitoria we approached a wood that was there. At the edge of this wood was a carriage which had been run into a ditch and in this carriage sat a little curly-headed child, playing quite innocently, and guarded by a huge dog, something after the way of a mastiff; at any rate it was the largest I have ever seen before or since. Besides this we found a large box inside the carriage containing doubloons. These were distributed amongst us. When we approached

---

95 The Royals simply followed the infantry attacks during the battle and only lost one man wounded at the Battle of Vitoria. Once the French routed, the cavalry moved forward to press them (the regimental history of the Royals states that they stopped some 9 miles on the road to Pamplona). Even if this is true, they did not move rapidly, as proven by the lack of prisoners taken. The regimental history also admits that a regular sale of prize horses, wines etc was held that night and the proceeds shared and that each subaltern gained 20 dollars and each private 11 dollars. The regiment was therefore clearly delayed in gaining spoil and this hampered the pursuit

it, the dog growled and stood guard over the child as if it was its protector. The child seemed quite pleased, and patted it. Captain Hulton[96] asked if any one of us dared attempt to rescue the child, but the dog growled so savagely that nobody responded in a hurry. However, I said if any of my companions would get some meat and engage the attention of the dog a short time, I would lift the child from the carriage. The suggestion turned out to be a good one, for the dog grew more tractable, and even came and eat the food from my comrades' hands. I fetched the child away and took it to Captain Hulton, who said, 'Well done, Smithies; you're a brave fellow, and always was; take this child to the rear, and give it to the first woman you meet, and tell her it is a present from me.' Captain Hulton was very well liked among the ladies – in fact he was what you may term –'quite the ladies' man' – and he knew that he had only to send it in his name to secure it every comfort. He was a great favourite of Wellington's too, and his lordship called him his 'fighting captain. 'I left my regiment, and, lifting the child into my saddle, put spurs to my horse, and galloped off towards the rear of our army, which consisted of all our baggage, wounded, women, and children. After I had gone some five or six miles, I came up with them, and the first lady I met was Sergeant Leek's wife[97], and to her I gave up the 'captain's present.' It was very fortunate I did so, for she had no children, and was a particular friend of the captain's; so the child was very well cared for. In a few months after, being face to face with the enemy on the top of the Pyrenees Mountains, our captain ordered myself and the men who had to do with getting the child and the money out of the carriage, to go into the French camp with a flag of truce. We did so; and I carried the child. I had never been directly in the enemy's camp before; but you may be sure they showed us the way back as soon as our business was done, and did not give us any time to go gaping about us. We made enquiries, and in a few hours we found out the father and mother of this child, and also gave them back their dog. He was an officer of high rank, and he told us he had been obliged to abandon the carriage, with their child, their dog, their money and valuables, and in fact everything they were possessed of.

    Of course we had speculated on receiving some reward for restoring the child, if we happened to find the parents, but we were greatly disappointed, for they did not look very grateful, and just coldly thanked us. We were going away – and they had not offered us anything – when one of my comrades turned round and began

---

96 Captain George Hulton, Royal Dragoons; he died of natural causes in 1814.

97 I believe this to be the wife of Sergeant Thomas Leech, who served in Captain Radclyffe's Troop at Waterloo.

to beg from the officer, telling him he was 'hard up'; but the Frenchman said he too was 'hard up,' for we had taken every dollar he had in the world. We gave it up as a bad job, and knowing we could not kick blood out of a stone; we left them and returned to our camp. Our conversation was carried on in French, as we had acquired a slight knowledge of the French and Spanish languages whilst in the Peninsula; but it would be 'broken-French' in a manner of speaking, same as their attempts at our language were 'broken-English.' Vitoria was fought on the 21st day of June; it was the longest day of the year. After the battle was over, and we were encamped, Wellington and his staff rode down our centre. As he was passing our quarters, I distinctly heard him say, in a joking sort of a manner, 'That though it had been the longest day in the year, it was about two hours too short.' And the general opinion expressed was that only the darkness saved the French army from annihilation on that day.

As I have said before, our army advanced towards the Pyrenees, and without attempting to go into minute particulars, I may say that I took part in the battles of San Sebastian, Orthes, Sorauren (twice), and many other places after we had crossed into France[98]. I cannot remember all names, as some of the words in the French language are such 'jawbreakers.'

I have told you about a man called Asker, who was in our regiment, and sometimes conducted prayer meetings when we were in cantonments. I recollect a rather amusing story he once told me whilst we were encamped in the Pyrenees, concerning his sister, who he described as a very handsome girl. His sister was walking out one day with two lady friends, when they met a young man, who it afterwards turned out had fallen over head and ears in love – at first sight – with Miss Asker. He made many inquiries as to who the young lady was, and was told by one of her companions 'Asker'. He felt rather annoyed at being told to 'Ask her,' so he inquired of another and was again told 'Asker'. He felt certain they were teasing him, and did not seek her company for a great length of time, when, by accident, it was explained to him, and I believe he lost no time in 'ask (ing) er,' and they got married. The young man, Asker, wrote several pieces whilst we were in Spain. He gave me a copy of them, and I learnt every word off by heart, and can recite them to this day, though I had not seen either a written or printed copy for more than fifty years until I called at Adam Gaunt's, in Jumbo, as I was

---

98 The cavalry were rested in the plains of Navarre as they were useless during the fighting in the Pyrenees and remained in the area of Sanguessa. The Royals did however help search for the wounded lying scattered after the twin battles of Sorauren. The regiment had no hand in the siege of San Sebastian, nor were they involved at the Battle of Orthes in the spring of 1814 as Smithie claims.

passing the other day, and they showed me the verses I knew so well. But I am getting away from my story; I may just mention that David Taylor[99], of Middleton, who was one of the Oxford Blues, paid me a visit in camp one day. It was about noon, and I was preparing dinner. I stood outside my tent kneading some dough in wine for a pudding, when I heard someone shout 'Smithies, heaw arta, lad,' and turning round I saw David. We had not seen each other for years, and we had to have a long talk over what we had gone through, and what our prospects were. Some of you seem to wonder that I should be using wine for kneading dough, but, as I said before, it was much more plentiful than water anywhere. We thought water a great luxury. Wellington had a deal to contend with his army after we had got into France. The inhabitants received us well enough, but the Spaniards in our army were burning to retaliate for the cruelty and rapacity of the French soldiery whilst they had been in the occupation of Spain. The Spaniards plundered a good deal, and did an immense amount of mischief on the first two days, but this was promptly put a stop to by Wellington, who ordered some of them to be shot, whilst others were sent back to Spain to be confined in prison till the close of the war. This step convinced the French peasantry that we had no desire to injure them, and many returned to their homes who had left on the approach of our army[100].

But when the French soldiers saw the inhabitants were returning to their homes, and thus placing themselves under British protection, they had the cowardliness to shoot them down, – aye, their own countrymen too! As there was hardly a soldier in the Spanish or Portuguese service who could not tell of a parent, a brother, or sister murdered by the French soldiers, the Spaniards or Portuguese talked of retribution and revenge, and looked forward to the plunder of France as just retaliation for all the misery the French had inflicted on Spain and Portugal. Wellington issued a proclamation to his army about the plundering, and as they continued their ravages, several were caught and hung. Several regiments of Spaniards were sent back to their own country for this offence. I heard a story at the time, which shows what a thirst for revenge some of them fostered. Some of our soldiers were strolling about the town when they heard loud screams. They ran in the direction from whence they appeared to come, when they found a poor old French peasant lying dead at the bottom of a garden. A bullet had passed through his head, and his thin grey hairs were dyed with

---

99 Private David Taylor of the Horse Guards served at Vitoria and Toulouse but was not at Waterloo.
100 Wellington made the decision to send most of his Spanish troops back to Spain despite the reduction in the size of his army because he feared reprisals by the French peasantry more.

his own blood. A Cacadore (Portuguese) rushed out and attempted to elude them. On entering they saw an old woman, the wife of the peasant, lying dead in the kitchen. The desperate Portuguese did not deny having committed these murders; he seemed to be mad: 'They murdered my father,' he said; 'they cut my mother's throat; they ravished my sister before my eyes; and I vowed would put to death the first French family that came into my hands. You may hang me if you will; but I have kept my oath, and I care not for dying.' He was hanged, and no fewer than eighteen others along with him, for having committed the like offence. They were hung up on branches of trees, so that the army might see the example they had made of the marauders. For a whole week such scenes as these were witnessed, scores were hung, and several regiments were disarmed. Adjutant General Pakenham detected two British soldiers plundering in Ascain, and he caused them to be hung on the two trees nearest to the spot, with papers affixed to their breasts detailing for what offence this summary justice was inflicted; and several officers were sent to England in disgrace, for not having repressed the conduct of their men.

Winter now set in with unusual severity, and the cold became so intense that the sentries were frozen to death very frequently. Perished with wet and cold, the troops began to show signs of discontent. The days were extremely hot, whilst the nights were piercingly cold and frosty. At times, too, the rain would come down in torrents, and coming through our canvass tents drove away all possibility of sleep; sometimes the worms would even come out of the ground when it became too wet for them. In such a night as this, it was weary work to wait the long dreary hours until daylight came, with a craving stomach, and, worse still, to find no better prospect than a bellyful of bullets for breakfast. Many of our sentries deserted to the enemy, from a fear or dread of the dead bodies they very often met with on their beat, and these men, who feared neither the French nor any human being, were seized with a kind of superstitious awe, and deserted their posts rather than act as a watch over the living, and amidst the dead! That both soldiers and sailors are superstitious it is well known; yet it is anything but pleasant to stand sentry on a stormy night beside a mangled dead carcase, as I have done scores of times. When the officer has been appointing sentries for the night, I have heard men say, when asked to stand guard near one of their fallen comrades, 'I don't care for living men, but for God's sake, sir, don't put me beside him.' One night I had a vision which I never shall forget. We had lain down on the ground to rest for the night, with our blankets over us, and our horses picketed near and ready for instant mount, when my horse laid down and rolled over me. I was very much hurt with it, and getting vexed I got up to give it a good kicking then saw my sister coming towards me, and she said these words: 'Jim, thi mother always told thee that as thea made thi bed, so theaw'd ha to lie' and then went out of sight. I was neither drunk nor dreaming when I saw this. It was very remarkable indeed that by the next mail I received a letter informing me of my sister's illness (of which I knew nothing whatever before) and death; and more remarkable still that the time of her death and the date exactly corresponded with the night I saw her, as I took particular notice of it. (The old veteran was always much affected when he related this incident.)

The battle of Nivelle was the first brisk engagement we took part in after we had crossed the borders of France. With the first break of day, a brisk cannonade announced that the battle had begun. About seven o'clock in the morning our artillery made some impression on the redoubts in front of Sarre, the soldiers of both columns of our centre leaping up, with a loud hurrah, and rushed to their points of attack; the left column against the Rhone, and the right columns against the redoubts and the village of Sarre. The Llight Division the 4th and 7th Divisions stormed all the entrenchments of the mountain. It was now eight o'clock, and the whole of our centre was united and established at the brow of La Petite Rhine. In a few minutes they reached the summit of the mountain, within twenty yards of the walls of the first fort. The soldiers and officers fairly gasped for breath; the former from the weight of their knapsacks and accoutrements, staggered and fell, and before they could recover their feet, were pierced with bullets, no more to rise. The first fort was carried, and the second was then attacked hand to hand, the French using their bayonets and the butt end of their rifles. One of our officers gallantly jumped into the second fort, and a French soldier thrust a bayonet through his handkerchief, fixing him to the wall, and then firing his piece which blew away the officer's collar, who immediately jumped up unhurt. Another officer, while clambering up the wall, received such a severe blow on the fingers with the butt end of a firelock, which compelled him to drop from his hold. Indeed they were so hard pressed, that several officers seized the dead soldiers' firelocks and fought with them like bludgeons. As the enemy rushed out of the second fort, a little athletic fellow, with red hair, one of our men, eagerly followed an officer; the Frenchman parried two of his thrusts, but finding his men were giving way, he turned suddenly round, and made off: our man, fearing his prey might escape, hurled his firelock at him; the bayonet pierced the Frenchman's body, when he fell heavily on his face with the weight of the musket, the bayonet still sticking in him. Another French officer stood up on the top of the wall, with both his eyes hanging on his cheeks, and not daring to move from his perilous position lest he should tumble down the precipice, some hundred feet in depth. Throughout the day such scenes as these were conspicuous. With the approach of night the firing ceased on our part. The victory, if any, was certainly ours, as we gained considerable ground, took many of their strongholds, and destroyed a great many of their men. The losses on both sides were very nearly equal, that of the French being 3,000, and ours 2,600.[101]

The rain began to descend in torrents, and thus put an end to operations, at least for a time. When we were not fighting, we were frequently fraternising with the French troops, and the friendly habits and generous intercourse which had long been established between our outposts and theirs were now again put into practice. During the short term of inaction that the inclemency of the weather had occasioned, one of these occurrences took place between our outposts and those of the French. A disposition had for some time been gaining ground with both armies to mitigate the miseries of warfare whenever it did not seem inconsistent with their duties. It even became so common that we could pass each other's outposts unmolested. The next day there being no firing between us and those in our front, three French officers, who seemed anxious to show how far good breeding and politeness could be carried on between the two nations, when war did not compel them to be unfriendly, brought a table and some chairs immediately in our front, not a hundred yards from our sentry, and drank wine, holding up their glasses as much as to say 'Your Health,' every time they drank. Of course we did not molest them, but allow them to have their frolic out. During the same day I saw the soldiers of the French, Portuguese, and English all plundering at the same time in one house. They plundered in perfect harmony, no one disturbing the other on account of his nation or colour. Indeed perfect confidence existed between us. The French used to get us things that we wanted from Bayonne, particularly brandy, which was both cheap and plentiful; and we, in return, gave them a little tea, of which some of them learned to be very fond. While our 5th Division was at Hasparen, the pickets of both armies avoided every appearance of hostility, it being an understood thing that they should not attack each other's outposts, for the purpose of gaining the paltry advantage of destroying fifty to a hundred men. Each of us occupied a hill, with sentries about 200 yards apart. The French, on one occasion pushed forward their videttes, and seemed as if their design was to trespass on neutral ground. The English captain reported this encroachment, and received orders not to allow it. On the following

---

101 The Battle of Nivelle, 10 November 1813, was an infantry affair in the mountains and the Royals were not engaged. According to Oman the Allied losses totalled 2,526 killed, wounded & missing; the French lost 4,321.

morning he observed that the French vidette had been advanced about fifty yards, and he thought it most advisable to seek an interview with the French captain. He sent a peasant who returned with a message that the commandant would wait on the English officer immediately, and in a few minutes the parties met on neutral ground. The Englishman stated his case, what were his orders, and that he had solicited an interview in order to avoid so 'mean' (so he thought) a proceeding as firing on a small vidette. The Frenchman expressed himself on the most flattering terms, and begged the Englishman would point out a situation agreeable to himself. A thorn bush about one hundred yards behind the spot upon which the French vidette was posted, was mentioned as equally advantageous for the security of the French picket. This suggestion was acted upon, the vidette being removed to the very place pointed out. The Frenchman expressed his satisfaction at the interview, and then produced a bottle of cognac, two or three officers on each side soon joined the party; a happy termination to the war was drunk; and the French officers said at parting, they trusted it would not bring into collision the parties who had met in so amicable a manner.

As we were crossing the Pyrenees we saw, not twenty yards in front of us, a wounded voltigeur extended on the ground, and a young comrade supporting him. The Frenchman never attempted to retreat; but smiled as we came up, as if he had been expecting us. 'Good morning,' he said, as soon as we had come up to him, 'I have been waiting for you, gentlemen. My poor friend's leg is broken by a shot, and I could not leave him until you arrived, lest some of those Portuguese brigands should murder him.' 'Pierre', he said, addressing the wounded man, 'Here are the brave English, and you will be taken care of. I will leave you [a] flask of water, and you will be succoured by our noble enemy.' 'Gentlemen, will you honour me by emptying this canteen. You will find it excellent, for I took it from a portly friar two days ago.' There was no need to repeat the invitation, and I set the example; the canteen passed from mouth to mouth, and the monk's brandy rapidly vanished. The young man was a recruit, and had only been in the French army a month; he replenished the flask with water from a spring close by, and after placing it in his comrade's hand bade him an affectionate farewell. He then bowed very gratefully to us, threw his musket over his shoulder, and trotted off to join his regiment, which he pointed out upon a distant height. He seemed never to contemplate the possibility of our detaining him as our prisoner, but there was about him so much kindness and confidence that not one of us dreamt of detaining him. I happened to hear of another case or two of the same sort. On one occasion a sentry of the 52nd, being posted within a few yards of a French sentry, made his enemy understand, in a sort of Spanish gibberish, that he was much in want of tobacco. The Frenchman, with great politeness, offered to supply his wants if he would give him money to buy some in the rear of his post; then a five franc piece was forked out, but, before given, it was necessary to have a guarantee for the fulfilment of the treaty. The Frenchman agreed to leave his firelock in pledge; but then another difficulty arose. The French sentry said, 'But who is to keep my post?' The Englishman easily solved that question by exclaiming, 'Oh, never mind that! I am the only one opposed to you, and I'll keep your post till you return. It afterwards appeared that the vivandiere[102] who sold the tobacco had also a bottle of brandy, and the change of the five-franc piece appeared too great a temptation to resist, and the 'military honour' of the Frenchman must have got drowned in it, for he was found dead drunk by his picket. He, of course, was asked where his firelock was, and who had it. His explanation was with difficulty believed; but on a communication between the officers of the opposing pickets, the preliminaries of an amicable treaty were duly exchanged and ratified, with a present of the tobacco. But the most amusing I have yet got to tell you. A daring fellow, an Irishman, named Tom Patten[103], performed a singular feat. At the barrier between the two pickets there was a rivulet, along which our lines of sentries were posted. To the right was a thick low wood, and during the cessation of hostilities our officers had again become intimate with those of the French, and the men had actually established a tariff in tobacco and brandy in the following ingenious manner: A large stone was placed in that part of the river screened by the wood, opposite to the French sentry, on which our people used to put a canteen with a quarter dollar, for which it was very soon filled with brandy. One afternoon, about dark, Tom had put down his canteen with the usual money in it, and retired, but though he returned several times, no canteen was there. He waited till the moon rose, but still he found nothing on the stone. When it was near morning Tom thought he saw the same sentry who was there when he put his canteen down; so he sprang across the stream, seized the unfortunate Frenchman, wrested his firelock from him, and actually shaking him out of his jacket, re-crossed, vowing he would keep them until he got his canteen of brandy, and brought them to the picket house. Two or three hours afterwards, just as we were about to fall in, an hour before daybreak, the sergeant came to say that a flag of truce was at the barrier; one of our people went down, and found the French officer of the picket in a state of

---

102 A French woman camp follower who sold supplies to the soldiers.

103 This story has been repeated elsewhere, but Smithie seems to indicate that the man was of his regiment. There was a Private Thomas Parton in the Royals at Waterloo, is this our man?

great alarm, saying that a most extraordinary circumstance had occurred (relating the adventure), and stating that if the sentry's firelock and accoutrements were not given back, his own commission would be forfeited, as well as the life of the poor sentry. A sergeant went to see if they were in the picket house, when Tom came up, scratching his head vigorously, and saying, 'I have them in pawn for a canteen of brandy and a quarter dollar,' at the same time giving his version of the story. The end of it was the Frenchman's firelock and accoutrements were returned, and Tom got his dollar and the brandy too[104].

I shall conclude my story by giving a short account of the battles of Toulouse, where we fought for seven days without intermission; the signing of the treaty of peace by which Napoleon was delivered up and sent in exile to Elba; the return of our army to England; Napoleon's escape from Elba; our departure for Belgium; the battle of Quatre Bras and Waterloo; and my return home again.

The day we first attacked them at Toulouse was on the 4th of April, 1814, and we could distinctly hear the bells ringing calling the inhabitants to mass, at the same time our bands were gaily playing 'The Grenadier's March' and 'The Downfall of Paris.' The morning being bright and beautiful, the inhabitants collected to witness the exciting scene. The peasants even volunteered their aid, and assisted in dragging the guns of the horse artillery up the banks. I am afraid the details of the battle would be too tedious, so it must suffice to say that Marshal Soult was forced to retreat, after a fight which lasted a week[105]. It was on Easter Sunday that we gave him a finishing touch and on the following day he evacuated Toulouse. Our army, with Wellington at its head, entered the town at twelve o'clock the same day, and the populace cheered him, and hailed him as their

---

104 These instances were talked of throughout the army and are often quoted, therefore it is impossible to be sure that they actually occurred when the Royals were present; although the story of the wounded Frenchman is new to me and could well have occurred during the Royals advance into France in March 1814. Because the country was not suitable for cavalry actions, the cavalry were left in the valley of the Ebro to recuperate from the rigours of the advance. The Royals stayed in the vicinity of Villafranca for the winter and only commenced their march into France on 2 March, passing Pamplona on 8 March, Irun 9 March, St Jean de Luz 13 March and Dax 18 March, and finally joining the army on its march to Toulouse.

105 Toulouse was invested on 23 March, but attacking it was not easy, being surrounded by heights and waterways which were heavily defended. After a number of incursions, Wellington launched an attack on the eastern heights, whilst the Royals, still attached to Hill's Corps watched proceedings whilst menacing the defenders of St Cyprien on the west. There were no casualties in the Royals at Toulouse at all.

deliverer. A lot of officials – who would be like aldermen here – came out to meet him, their mayor having decamped with Soult.

About five o'clock the same evening, Colonel Cooke and a French officer arrived at Wellington's head quarters from Paris with despatches announcing the abdication of Napoleon Bonaparte and the restoration to the throne of Louis XVIII. It was the Frenchman's duty also to make this communication to Soult, but that general at first refused to believe the news. However, on receiving another official intimation to the same effect he at once made preparations for entering into an armistice with Wellington. Our loss in this celebrated battle was very considerable, but that of the French must have been enormous. Wellington proceeded to Paris, and after Napoleon had been safely ensconced in Elba, the Duke returned, and we marched 'on our journey home' through Paris to Calais[106], at which place we embarked for Dover, where we arrived in a few days after, having been absent from Old England nearly six years[107].

Nothing important occurred after we arrived home, for a short time: we had all to see our friends and receive their congratulations, of course. We however were not allowed to be quiet long, for the news came that Napoleon had escaped from Elba, and we were again called to arms. We set sail for Belgium in May 1815[108], and the two armies met again on the field of Waterloo. The British force sent into Belgium amounted to something like 30,000 men, and about this number took part in the battle of Waterloo; our allies were the Belgians, Hanoverians, Dutch, Nassauers, Brunswickers, (who did not do much good, as they turned on their heels when coming up with the enemy,) and Prussians (who were little better).[109] All the reinforcements and supplies were sent from England by way of Ostend. The whole of the line of cantonments was of considerable extent, forming a large portion of the circle, of which Brussels was the centre. At this time Brussels was thronged with visitors, comprising many of the fashionable nobles of England.

---

106 The cavalry were marched across France to Calais to reduce the shipping needs at Bordeaux, however the march did not proceed through Paris itself.

107 The Royals landed at Dover on 19 July 1814 having been abroad for a month short of five years. The regiment was sent to Bristol and later to Exeter, from whence Troops were detached to Truro and Taunton.

108 The regiment received orders for Belgium on 21 April and they marched via Canterbury to Ramsgate where they embarked between 13 & 16 May. The regiment marched via Ghent to Ninove and the surrounding villages. The regiment was brigaded with the 2nd Dragoons or Scots Greys and 6th Enniskillen Dragoons commanded by Major General the honourable Sir William Ponsonby.

109 Smithies' criticism of the Brunswickers and especially the Prussians is unfair.

Grand dinners, balls, and concerts were given almost every night, and the theatres were crowded with brilliant assemblies, whilst all was life and bustle in camp. In every farmer's house, or labourer's cottage, were to be seen three or four and sometimes more of our soldiers. They all seemed to make themselves at home, particularly the Highlanders who in some instances might be found attending to their host's shop, rocking a cradle, or doing little odd jobs about the house. I may say that the great part of our army was composed of raw recruits, drafts from the militia, and soldiers who had never stood fire, as many of the regiments that took part in the Peninsular campaign were kept at home; whilst the French force, which numbered, I should say, nearly 100,000 men, was composed of hardy veterans, who had borne the brunt of battle before. The preparations for battle were made on a very extensive scale; for the first time ever known in our army, the cavalry were ordered to grind the backs of their swords, as, so our Captain Clarke said, 'we should have to use both sides.' It was thought by the men that this order had been given because we had to contend with a large number of French cuirassiers, who had steel armour, and through this we should have to cut[110]. During this time Napoleon had not been idle. At the call of their emperor, his veteran soldiers, who were familiar with war, flocked to his standard. On the 8th of June his army set out from Paris, and reached Avesnes, a town on the north east of France, on the 13th, their line of march being characterised by their propensities for plundering, murdering and leaving in desolation every town, and village they passed through. They cut whole fields of corn down to supply thatch for their camp huts, and forage for their horses. About tea time on the 15th, information was brought into our camp that the French would shortly be upon us, and Wellington issued his orders accordingly. At ten o'clock the same evening another communication was sent to Wellington by Marshal Blucher, stating that the French had crossed the river Sambre, above Avesnes, and orders were given for a portion of our army to move towards Quatre Bras.

It was past midnight when the drums suddenly beat to arms in Brussels, and the trumpet's call was heard in every street of the sleeping city. I will be bound to say there never was such a Babel of sounds heard in Brussels before – people were crying and making all kinds of pitiful noises, whilst the soldiers were tramping about through the city, and guns and carriages were rattling over the stony streets. Wellington left us and proceeded to take command of that portion of our army

---

110 It was impossible for swords to penetrate the cuirassiers steel body armour, but it was not immune to musket and cannon fire.

that had gone to Quatre Bras. My regiment was amongst those left behind[111]. The battle of Quatre Bras, as you all know, was fought the day but one[112] before Waterloo, and it was very toughly contested; the Belgians fled in great disorder when they were ordered to face the French cavalry[113]. During the night of the 16th, Wellington received information from Blucher that he had been defeated at Ligny, upon which our army was ordered to fall back and concentrate on what will always be known as the field of Waterloo. The night before the battle of Waterloo was one of the most dreary and cheerless that could possibly be conceived, for besides there being a very high wind, the rain poured down in torrents, and loud crashes of thunder, with vivid flashes of lightning, lasted throughout this memorable night. We had to rest on the cold wet ground, or amongst the dripping corn, which I can assure you was anything but pleasant. The morning broke slowly and gloomily, and it was not long before we were up and shaking ourselves. Our first duty was to give our arms and trappings a thorough cleaning, for the rain had made them quite rusty, after which we took breakfast, and the trumpets then sounded for us to assemble with our respective regiments. I will give a description of the field, if I can.

The whole length of our line would be about a mile and a half, that of the French, probably two miles. The Brussels road ran at right angles through both armies; forming the centre of each. On this road, as it were, in one line, were the villages of Mont St. Jean and two farm houses, called La Haye Sainte and La Belle Alliance; and the only other place I have need to mention is Hougoumont, which is advanced a short way in front of nearly the right of our position. The position of our allied army was in a forest on the Brussels road, near to Mont St. Jean; and at Waterloo. That of the French was directly opposite us on a range of heights. La Haye Sainte was a farm house, with a very large orchard at the back of it; Hougoumont was an old fashioned country house, with a farm-yard and other outbuildings on one side; on the other a chapel and observatory, with a brick wall round it, and a little wood in front[114]. Our army was divided in two lines, with the cavalry in the rear. My regiment was brigaded with the 6th Enniskillen Dragoons and the Scots Greys. The French army was marshalled in two lines with a reserve.

---

111 It should be remembered that the Royals were not at Brussels, but at Ninove.

112 Two days before on 16 June.

113 The Belgian/Dutch troops fought bravely at Quatre Bras, allowing time for Wellington's infantry to arrive.

114 Smithie makes it clear that he visited the battlefield again a while after the battle, therefore he had better knowledge than most soldiers of the complete layout of the battlefield.

As I said before, directly after we had finished our breakfast the word of command was given 'Stand to your arms, the French are on the move.' Bonaparte took up his position near La Belle Alliance: and about eleven o'clock his brother Jerome began the battle by an attack on Hougoumont, where some of the Guards were garrisoned. The number of men who moved on Hougoumont under Jerome Bonaparte was 3,000, who advanced to the fight with loud cheers and shouts, but a brigade of our artillery placed its guns in such a position that they fired murderous volleys into the French ranks, sweeping down whole columns at a time. But in a short time the French brought one of their heavy brigades of artillery, and very soon silenced ours. The French infantry then drove in the Nassauers, and obtained possession of the [town?] and drove the assailants back, and recovered the wood and the garden. About 8,000 men on both sides were killed in the attack and defence of this place alone; our Guards lost more than 800 men. The battle, which had hitherto been confined to Hougoumont, now became general throughout. The whole of the enemy's artillery opened on our line, principally on the right and centre. I cannot give any particulars of other portions of our army after this, as our regiment was too busily engaged in its immediate front.

During the progress of the attack on Hougoumont, and the cannonade which had been opened from our artillery, a large portion of the French force advanced on our centre and left, apparently with the intention of piercing the one and turning the other, and thus to cut off our communication by the high road to Brussels, as well as to prevent our junction with the Prussians. As soon as their skirmishers opened fire on a Belgian-Dutch brigade[115], the troops fled in the utmost confusion, and as they passed our lines at the top of their speed, our men hissed and hooted them. At the same time the enemy attacked the farm of La Haye Sainte, a Hanoverian regiment was sent to reinforce the men at that post, but they were so alarmed at the appearance of the French cuirassiers that they hurriedly took flight; but, being overtaken by the 'men in steel armour,' they were nearly all cut down[116]. On the flight of this cowardly brigade, General Picton prepared to meet the enemy who were advancing 20,000 men against him, whilst he had only about 3,000. The French came on like a swarm, cheering as they advanced, when Picton ordered his men to give them a volley, and then 'Charge.' He had scarcely given the command to 'Charge, charge,' when he was struck down lifeless by a musket ball which had been shot through his head.

---

115 The brigade of Bijlandt.

116 This describes a later incident involving the 5th Line Battalion K.G.L.

The French infantry retreated before Picton's bayonet charge, for the men had become maddened because their leader was killed. The French cuirassiers ascended the hill and were about to charge Picton's little band, when the Earl of Uxbridge, seeing this, ordered our brigade; my regiment, the Scots Greys, and the Enniskilleners to charge them.

The 'cuirassiers', you will recollect, had coats of steel, whilst we had no such protection; and then again their swords were much longer, which made it greater odds who would come victorious out of the fray. On we rushed at each other, and when we met the shock was terrific. We wedged ourselves between them as much as possible, to prevent them from cutting, and the noise of the horses, the clashing of swords against their steel armour, can be imagined only by those who have heard it. There were some riders who had caught hold of each other's bodies – wrestling fashion – and fighting for life, but the superior physical strength of our regiment soon showed itself, and we drove them from the ridge. You may perhaps think it strange I say nothing of what I did myself in this charge; I did [the] same as the rest, and got through as well as I could, I had many a hard tussel, and might have had to knock under, if I had not been a superior swordsman. It was desperate work, indeed, cutting through their steel armour. We were next ordered to charge a whole regiment of French Lancers, who looked, if possible, a still uglier enemy than their 'coated' brethren. The lance was fastened to their foot, and when we neared them, they sent it out with all their might; and if the man at which they aimed did not manage to parry the blow, it was all over with him. It was just this way: if the Englishman managed to throw aside his opponent's lance, he could cut at the Frenchman before the latter could recover his sword, but if the lance was not parried, it felled its victim with unerring certainty. Now a dexterous swordsman scarcely feared facing these lancers, as he felt a sort of confidence in himself that by a well aimed blow he could in a manner disarm his enemy, and then have him at his mercy. Our brigade, under Sir William Ponsonby, then galloped through the intervals made by the wheeling back of Pack's brigade, and dashed into the mass of French infantry columns, and mowing them down like grass, dispersed them. Whilst they fell back we continued to press them, when one of them turned round, fired his gun, and shot me on the bridle hand, the left. I turned round and found my regiment had been called back, and being severely wounded, I made the best of my way back towards the rear. I failed in getting back to my regiment, and several French hussars seeing me galloping about, gave me chase, and as I refused to stop, they fired many shots at me, but without effect. They then fired at my horse, and succeeded in bringing it to the ground by a shot in the hip joint.

I dismounted, and prepared to surrender myself a prisoner; but instead of taking my sword honourably, they cut at me, and it was only by a very quick movement that I saved myself. They at last took my sword, and making my horse get upon its feet, they placed a wounded Frenchman on its back, and I was forced to walk by its side, although my wound was as bad as his. As we went along through the standing corn, I saw hundreds of Frenchmen hiding, and troops of horsemen driving them into the field. We came to a brook, and in leaping it I got hold of my guard's bridle, and tried to throw him off his horse into the stream, and nearly effected my design; he saw this, and when he had waded through, he rode towards me and cut at me fiercely, and would have killed me, had not another Frenchman interfered. We at last got to their rear, just as the French began to retreat. They turned all the English prisoners into a yard, and we were driven in like sheep. But this place got too hot for them, and the little fat French officer shouted out in his language, 'Save yourselves.' We all ran out in a body down a road leading towards France, still being guarded as prisoners, of course. The cowardly Frenchmen were mortified that their army was retreating, and meted their vengeance on the poor wounded prisoners. I saw many a one cut through with the sword, and rolled over into the ditch. A Middleton man, whom I knew very well, was amongst the lot, and because he was unable to go on at the speed they wanted him, a Frenchman cut at him and took off his nose and one side of his face, which I saw fall in the mud; and in trying to save him, I very nearly met a worse fate. Another poor fellow who was unable to walk any further, as he had been shot in the knee, was run through and rolled over on one side. I might recite a score of such cases; all along the route the French exercised the greatest cruelty towards us, and acted more like barbarians than anything I know. The total rout of the French cannot be described; all were hurrying in the greatest possible confusion by every conceivable road towards their own country. At night we were turned into a convent yard. My wound had not been attended to yet, and all the doctoring it had received was from a piece of my shirt which I tore from my back to wrap round my hand, which was half blown off. The place or yard was as muddy as possible, and there was only some slight covering at one end like a hay shed, that would not shelter one half of us. A great fire was made at night, and it was a curious sight to see us squatted round it; some were laughing and quite gay, whilst others were groaning under the most excruciating pain from their wounds. To secure a resting place for the night, I carried a lot of sticks from the fire, and placing them close together on the ground, in two or three rows with an extra row or two at one end for a pillow, I contrived to get, if not a comfortable bed, at least a dry one. I had not much difficulty in getting to sleep, especially after I had had a 'pull' at a friendly Frenchman's brandy flask, and I don't think I ever had a sounder night's sleep in my life. In the morning, just at daylight, I was suddenly awakened by two Frenchmen, who were probing my sides with their bayonets to see if I would stir, and I found I was the last man in the place. I was marched out and soon came up with the rest of the prisoners. Nothing particular occurred until we halted at noon, when Napoleon paid a visit to the English soldiers who were his prisoners[117]. He came and spoke to most of us. He said something in French to an Oxford Blue, who stood near to me, and on leaving him they shook hands; he then came to me, but when he offered me his hand I cursed him, and (showing him my wounded hand), said that but for him I should not have been hurt in that manner. I refused his proffered hand, and turned my back on him. He seemed to think his dignity insulted, and gave me a scornful look that I shall never forget. He made some sort of a remark to the Oxford Blue about my conduct, as he was passing him, but I did not care, and did not feel particularly anxious to know what it was he had said. Napoleon left the 'pen' we had been put in, and dinner was served out.

We were not allowed to lose any time with eating, and word coming that the Prussians (who had taken up the pursuit after the English had left the field) were pressing forward, we were again put on the march, and so closely were the French now pursued, that they had quite as much to do to mind themselves, let alone their prisoners. Many of our men had escaped during the day, and towards night as we were passing over a bridge, a German officer (a prisoner) and myself concealed ourselves under it until our captors were out of sight. We took the best way we could, and set off for Brussels, depending on the liberality of the inhabitants for our subsistence until we reached there, which we did after a march of about ten days. I parted from my German friend, and obtained admittance into the hospital, where my wound was examined for the first time. The doctor, an Englishman, said that from its long neglected state he expected mortification would set in, and to prevent this proposed to amputate my arm. I strongly objected to this, thinking I might as well lose my life as my arm. Under the care of the doctor, however, it happily took a turn for the better, and in about nine or ten days I was liberated. I then set about making preparations for returning home, but before leaving Brussels, two English literary gentlemen found me out, and engaged me to accompany them to the field of battle. We went in a coach and pair, and I explained the various points of attack, where I had been wounded and taken prisoner, the field in which Sir William Ponsonby was killed, where Wellington's

---

117 It is unlikely that this person was Napoleon who had quickly removed himself from the routing troops; it is more likely to have been a senior French marshal or general.

and Napoleon's respective headquarters had been, and many other things which were no doubt interesting to them. Although it was only about a month after the battle, the ground on which it had been fought was being ploughed ready for tilling. There were still many cannon by the roadsides and hedge bottoms, which could not be easily removed. These gentlemen told me that they were writing a history of the battle, and gave me their address to call upon them in London, but I unfortunately lost it, and could never remember the name of the place where I was to have gone. To make a long story short, I may say that after returning to Brussels I obtained my pass, when I set sail for England, and arrived in London in the beginning of August, 1815. I joined my regiment, but nothing worth mentioning occurred until I received my discharge, which was not long after I returned home. As we were on the march northward, we passed the seat of our favourite captain, Lord Montagu. He invited us all to his house, and we partook of a splendid dinner on the lawn in front of his mansion, for it was a beautiful day. It was the last time I ever saw his lordship, though he lived a great many years after. After I got to my regiment I found many of my former comrades missing, many had been killed, and many more crippled so that they were not allowed to remain with the regiment. At the battle of Waterloo we had lost 88 men in killed, and as many were wounded in our regiment[118]. Captain Clarke had taken an eagle when we charged the French infantry at the time I was wounded[119]. I returned home, and it was quite a treat to hear the old bells of St. Leonard's[120] ringing so sweetly; I had often thought of them when I had been in battle, and at times I even fancied I heard them. After returning from the wars I settled down, got married[121], and have reared a large family. It is somewhat strange, but it is true nevertheless, that for many years successively my nose bled on the 18th of June, the anniversary of

---

118 The return published in 'A Near Observer' states the losses of the Royals as 4 officers killed, 9 wounded and 1 missing (actually killed); 86 men killed, 88 wounded and 9 missing.

119 Captain Clarke (later Kennedy-Clarke) and Corporal Stiles captured the eagle of the 105th Ligne, Stiles was given an ensigncy.

120 St Leonard's, Middleton, is the 15th Century parish church. It still retains parts of the original Norman church originally built on the site.

121 The records of St Leonards show that a James Smithies of Tonge was baptised 6 May 1787. The only marriage I can discover in Lancashire (between 1810-1850) is for a James Smithies and Alice Barlow both of Tonge on 3 May 1829 at St Mary the Virgin at Prestwich is this our man? If so this couple baptised Ann on 13 July 1830 and Thomas on 20 May 1832 at St Leonards. If there were further children they could have been baptised elsewhere, although St Michaels did not open until 1839.

the battle of Waterloo. The Duke of York gave me my medal, and said, 'You have on many occasions shown your bravery; here is your medal for Waterloo which you have gained with so much honour, and I hope that you will preserve it.' It was twenty years after that I received my Peninsular medal, which is of silver, and ornamented by three clasps, bearing the inscriptions, 'Bussaco' 'Fuentes d'Onoro,' and 'Vitoria',[122] being the three principal engagements I took part in, although I ought to have had clasps for Salamanca, the battles in the Pyrenees, Toulouse, and many other engagements.

I have now come to the end of my story, and I hope you have been pleased with it. I will conclude by reciting you a few verses on the battle of Waterloo:

>The ancient sons of Britain
>Were all great men it's said,
>And we in future story
>Shall shine as great as they.
>Our noble fathers, gallant sons,
>Shall conquer every foe,
>And long shall fame their names proclaim
>That fought at Waterloo.
>At ten o'clock on Sunday
>This bloody fray began,
>Which raged hot from that moment
>Till setting of the sun.
>My pen, I'm sure, can't half relate
>The glory of that day;
>We fought the French at Waterloo,
>And made them run away.
>
>Brave Wellington commanded us
>All on that glorious day,
>Where many a valiant Briton fell
>I sorry am to say.
>And many a thousand soldiers bold
>Lay bleeding in their gore

---

[122] James Smithies was even confused over his medal; for his General Service Medal for the Peninsular did have three clasps, but they were for Fuentes d'Onoro, Vitoria and Toulouse. His claim for Bussaco had some merit as the regiment was no more engaged at Vitoria, but did gain a clasp for their action there. He was certainly not at Salamanca or the battles in the Pyrenees, however.

Upon that day at Waterloo
When thundering cannons roared.

Our cavalrymen they did advance
With true and valiant hearts,
Our infantry, and artillery,
Did nobly play their parts;
And as Britons their resolve was
Never to quit that field,
Until the boasting proud Monsieur
They'd conquered and made yield.

The French dogs made a bold attack
In front of Mont St. Jean,
Three of their best battalions thought
The summit then to gain.
But Britons there received them
With hearts both true and stout,
When Sir William with his brigade
Soon put them to the rout.

As for Sir William Ponsonby,
With pain I have to say,
When leading on his heavy dragoons
Did meet his fate that day.
In front of his brigade he fell,
Which grieved my heart full sore,
I saw him lie as I passed by,
Like many a thousand more.

The cuirassiers like lions fought,
For they had coats of steel,
Being thus secured, they did advance,
Thinking to make us yield;
But our dragoons with sword in hand,
Did cut their armour through,
And show that day at Waterloo
What Britons only do.

Napoleon, like a bantam cock,
Was mounted on a car,
You might imagine he would be thought,
Great Mars, the God of War.
Raised up aloft that day he stood,
And loudly he did crow,
But dropped his wings and turned his tail
To us at Waterloo.

The valiant Duke of Brunswick[123]
Fell in the field that day,
And many more brave officers
In that terrific fray;
And many thousand soldiers bold
Lay weltering in their gore
Upon that day at Waterloo,
When thundering cannons roared.

The gallant Prince of Orange's Hussars
The right wing did command,
And sure a Prince more valiant
Ne'er took a sword in hand;
His Highness wounded was that day,
Charging the haughty foe,
And history will record his deeds
That day at Waterloo.

Our noble General Paget,
Marquis of Anglesea,
Upon that day he did command
The whole British cavalry;
His valour was most conspicuous shown
Wherever he did go,
He lost a limb whilst charging them
That day at Waterloo.

---

123 He was actually killed at Quatre Bras on 16 June.

Brave General Hill[124], so much renowned,
Commanded our left wing,
And with our British hearts so bold
Destruction he did bring.
As Hector-like he did behave,
Where thousands we laid low,
In verse sublime his deeds shall shine
That day at Waterloo.

When Napoleon he did perceive
That the victory we had won,
He did lament in bitter terms,
Crying, 'My darling son,
'I will set off for Paris straight
'And have him crowned also,
'Before they hear of my defeat
On the plains of Waterloo.'

Now, unto George, our gracious King,
My voice I mean to raise,
Likewise to the Prince Regent,
I mean to sing his praise.
The Duke of York and family,
And Wellington, you know,
And the soldiers, too, that bled that day
On the plains of Waterloo.

But let us raise our voice and praise
To him that the victory gave,
And may we still remember him
As long as we do live.
But to God alone all praise be given,
That fought for us, you know,
And gave to Britons victory
On the plains of Waterloo.

---

124 It was Picton who commanded the left wing.

Like many old and worthy veterans, who have fought and bled to uphold the honour and glory of their country, our hero was extremely proud of wearing his medals on 'pension-days' and other holidays. For a great length of time he was in the habit of taking a daily walk, and, although so far advanced in age, he thought it a mere trifle to set out on a journey which would necessitate his travelling eight or ten miles. On Friday, the 3rd day of January in this year, he met with an untimely death. About ten o'clock in the morning he left home with the intention of paying a visit to one of his daughters residing at Heywood. It appears that instead of going by the ordinary road, he struck across the tramway connected with the 'Nancy' Colliery' in Hopwood, and when walking up by the side of the rails was overtaken by a coal wagon, knocked down, and his left arm almost severed from the body. He had been very deaf for some years, and the men in charge of the wagon stated that they used every endeavour to warn him of the danger, but in vain. He was conveyed home, where he died about five o'clock in the afternoon of the same day. He was interred in St. Michael's Churchyard, Tonge[125], on the 8th, and, in accordance with his oft expressed wish, the following inscription has been placed upon his tombstone:

> IN MEMORY OF JAMES SMITHIES,
> FORMERLY OF H. M. FIRST ROYAL DRAGOONS,
> An old veteran of Portugal, Spain, France, and Waterloo,
> Who died January 3rd, 1868,
> IN THE 81ST YEAR OF HIS AGE.
> May he rest in peace.

---

125 St Michael's of Tonge-cum-Alkrington was built in 1839.

BIBLIOGRAPHY

Ainslie Gen., *The Historical Record of the First or The Royal Regiment of Dragoons*, London 1887

Anon, *Army Lists*, Various

Anon, *The Military Calendar*, London 1820

Burnham & McGuigan, *The British Army Against Napoleon*, Barnsley 2010

Chandler D, *Dictionary of The Napoleonic Wars*, London 1979

Hall JA, *History of the Peninsular War Vol VIII*, London 1998

Nafziger & Park, *The British Military*, Canada 1983

Oman Sir C., *A History of The Peninsular War*, London 1930

Oman Sir C., *Wellington's Army 1809-14*, London 1913

PREVIOUS AND FORTHCOMING PUBLICATIONS BY GARETH GLOVER

Voices of Thunder, UPSO Press August 2003

Letters from The Battle of Waterloo. Unpublished correspondence by allied officers from the Siborne papers, Greenhill Books May 2004

Memoirs of John Dayes, Paymaster Sergeant 5th Foot 1799-1822, Ken Trotman 2004

Recollections of my life including Service at Waterloo – Colonel George Blathwayt 23rd Lt Dragoons, Ken Trotman 2004

Reminiscences of Waterloo – The correspondence between Henry Leathes and Alexander Mercer G Troop RHA, Ken Trotman 2004

Wellington's Lieutenant, Napoleon's Gaoler – The Peninsula and St Helena. Letters and journals of Sir George Ridout Bingham 53rd Foot, Pen & Sword 2005

The Corunna diary of Captain C A Pierrepoint, Ken Trotman 2005

The Expedition to Walcheren 1809 By 2nd Captain Henry Light RA, Ken Trotman 2005

Letters from Egypt & Spain by Lt Col C Morland 12th then 9th Light Dragoons, Ken Trotman 2005

My Military Career by Lieutenant George Bourne 85th Foot, 1804-1818, Ken Trotman 2006

A Narrative of The Battles of Quatre-Bras And Waterloo; With the Defence of Hougoumont By Matthew Clay, Ken Trotman 2006

Ensign Carter's Journal 1812 30th Foot, Ken Trotman 2006

The Letters of 2nd Captain Charles Dansey RA 1806-13, Ken Trotman, 2006

A Life Guardsman in Spain, France and At Waterloo, the memoirs of Sergeant Major Thomas Playford 2nd Life Guards 1810-30, Ken Trotman 2006

Waterloo Letters, the 1815 letters of Lieutenant John Hibbert 1st King's Dragoon Guards, Ken Trotman 2007

The Diary of a Veteran, The diary of Sergeant Peter Facey, 28th Foot 1803-19, Ken Trotman 2007

From Corunna to Waterloo- The journals and letters of Major Edwin Griffiths and Captain Frederick Philips 15th (Kings) Hussars 1801-16, Greenhill Feb 2007

A Hellish Business, The Letters of Captain Charles Kinloch 52nd Foot, Ken Trotman 2007

The Letters Of Captain George Henry Dansey 88th Foot 1804-1814, Ken Trotman 2007

A Staff Officer in the Peninsula, the Letters of Lt Col James Stanhope 1810-15, Ken Trotman 2008

A Short Account of the Life and Adventures of Private Thomas Jeremiah, Royal Welch Fusiliers 1812-1837, including his experiences at the Battle of Waterloo, Ken Trotman 2008

The Waterloo diary of Captain James Naylor, 1st King's Dragoon Guards, 1815-16, Ken Trotman 2008

A Young Gentleman at War, The Letters of Captain the Honourable Orlando Bridgeman 1st Foot Guards, In the Peninsula and At Waterloo 1812-15, Ken Trotman 2008

A Guards Officer in the Peninsula and at Waterloo. The Letters of Captain George Bowles, Coldstream Guards 1807-1819, Ken Trotman 2008

The Military adventures of Private Samuel Wray, 61st Foot 1796-1815, Ken Trotman 2009

'It all culminated at Hougoumont'. The letters of Captain John Lucie Blackman 2nd Battalion Coldstream Guards, 1812-15, Ken Trotman 2009

With the Staff in Spain and Portugal. The letters of Robert Cooke, Army Pay Corps 1811-14, Ken Trotman 2009

Recollections of the Scenes of which I was Witness in the Low Countries & France in the Campaigns of 1814 and 1815 and the Subsequent Occupation of French Flanders. The Journal and Letters of the Reverend George Griffin Stonestreet 1814-16, Ken Trotman 2009

The Waterloo Archive – previously unpublished letters and journals from the Waterloo Campaign. Volume 1 British Sources, Frontline January 2010

Campaigning in Spain and Belgium. The letters of Captain Thomas Charles Fenton, 4th Dragoons & Scots Greys, 1809-15, Ken Trotman 2010

The Waterloo Archive – previously unpublished letters and journals from the Waterloo Campaign. Volume 2 German Sources, Frontline 2010

The Texas Papers, A Collection of Peninsular War Letters Written by various Senior British & Portuguese Officers held at the Woodson Research Centre, Rice University, Texas, Ken Trotman 2010

The Peninsular Diary of Captain John F Ewart, 52nd Light Infantry, 1811-12, Ken Trotman 2010

Eyewitness to the Peninsular War and Waterloo: The Letters and Journals of James Hamilton Stanhope 1808 to 1815, Pen & Sword November 2010

An Eloquent Soldier, The Peninsular War Journals of Lieutenant Charles Crowe of the Inniskillings, 1812-14, Frontline February 2011

Memoir of the Waterloo Campaign, 1815, by Lieutenant Colonel William Fielding, Coldstream Guards, Ken Trotman 2011

Captain Thomas Edwardes-Tucker's Peninsular Diary, 23rd (Royal Welch Fusiliers) Regiment of Foot, 1813-14 A.D.C to Sir Thomas Picton, Ken Trotman 2011

FORTHCOMING

The Waterloo Archive – previously unpublished letters and journals from the Waterloo Campaign. Volume 3 British Sources, Frontline, September 2011

The Waterloo Archive – previously unpublished letters and journals from the Waterloo Campaign. Volume 4 British Sources, Frontline, April 2012

Wellington's Voice, The candid letters of Lieutenant Colonel John Fremantle, Coldstream Guards 1808-1821, Frontline, February 2012

Letters from an Officer of the Corps of Engineers, from the British Army in Holland, Belgium & France to his Father, from the latter end of 1813 to 1816. The letters of First Lieutenant John Sperling Royal Engineers, Ken Trotman, Late 2011

The Diary of Ensign William Gavin 71st Foot 1806-15, Ken Trotman, Summer 2012

Seven Years on the Peninsula. The memoirs of Private Alexander Reed, 47th (Lancashire) Foot 1806-17, Ken Trotman Summer 2012